Guidelines for Reports by Autopsy Pathologists

T0234001

Guidelines for Reports by Autopsy Pathologists

Vernard Irvine Adams, MD
Author

Chief Medical Examiner, Hillsborough County, Florida
and
Department of Pathology and Cell Biology, University of South
Florida, Tampa, Florida, USA

 Humana Press

Author
Vernard Irvine Adams
Chief Medical Examiner Hillsborough County
Department of Pathology and
Cell Biology
University of South Florida
Tampa, FL 33617
USA

ISBN: 978-1-61737-900-0   e-ISBN: 978-1-60327-473-9

Printed on acid-free paper

9 8 7 6 5 4 3 2 1

springer.com

Preface

Guidelines for Reports by Autopsy Pathologists is intended to help the autopsy pathologist produce reports that communicate well. Having evolved from a collection of faculty critiques of the autopsy reports, summary and opinion reports, scene reports, and death certificates produced by residents in anatomic pathology and fellows in forensic pathology, the book emphasizes topics that have been troublesome for trainees. For clinicians, the medical record describes their work product. For autopsy pathologists, the written report *is* the work product and demands an accordingly higher standard of composition. Most reports produced by pathologists can be divided into objective and subjective elements, or, in other words, findings and opinions. The pathologist must have a clear understanding of the linkage between the two.

When composing a report, the autopsy pathologist should serve the goal of communicating to the parties who will read the report, namely, the case pathologist him- or herself (at a later date), attorneys, the family of the decedent, and other physicians. I believe that careless and imprecise thinking leads to sloppy language, and that sloppy language leads to careless and imprecise thinking. In my experience, pathologists who learn how to clearly express and organize their findings and opinions in a written format make more detailed and focused observations at the autopsy table.

In order to make cogent observations at the autopsy table, a pathologist must be a master of what the British call *morbid anatomy.* Morphological lesions cannot be adequately described if the pathologist cannot name the affected anatomical structures. Therefore, many of the guidelines are concerned with creating descriptions of lesions that are informed by a full understanding of anatomy.

Just as a sound knowledge of anatomy is essential to making the observations that go into the autopsy protocol, a sound knowledge of the mechanisms of death, that is, pathophysiological derangements, is necessary to make opinions concerning the cause, mechanism, and manner of death. An autopsy pathologist cannot be content merely to attach labels to morphological lesions. The pathologist, like a clinician, must think correlatively and base opinions on the totality of the circumstances, history, autopsy findings, and laboratory tests. This necessity informs the guidelines on opinion reports, which cover not only the report format, but also the logical process by which a pathologist forms opinions. For the purposes of vital records registration, physicians communicate with the Health Department through death certificates. A death certificate is essentially a highly formatted table of data. Unlike prose reports, which have no constraints on length, the spaces on a death certificate demand brevity. As a logical extension of the part on opinion reports, this book includes a section on completion of death certificates. Also included is a short section on record retention. "Record retention" is a term of art for the *scheduled destruction* of records. This section will be of interest to pathologists with administrative responsibility for an autopsy service. In *Guidelines for Reports by Autopsy Pathologists*, *pathologist* means any physician who performs autopsies, and is meant to include resident pathologists, hospital pathologists, and forensic pathologists. *Medical examiner* is the term used in this book for a physician who is a medicolegal officer charged with determining the cause of death. That physician may or may not be a pathologist, depending on the state jurisdiction, and in some states may be elected and carry the title of "coroner." Thus, the term *pathologist* finds heavy use in the section on autopsy reports, and the term *medical examiner* is used mostly in the section on death certification and record retention.

Vernard Irvine Adams
Tampa, Florida

Acknowledgments

Doctors Jurgen Ludwig, Keith Holley, William Edwards, Paul Belau, Joseph Davis, Charles Wetli, Brian Blackbourne, Charles Hirsch, Rebecca Hamilton, Laura Hair, Daniel Shultz, Russell Vega, Robert Lyon, Scott Kornman, Suzanne Utley, Scott McCormick, Vera Volnikh, Cecilia Rosales, and Kisha Mitchell helped to shape the author's concepts about report writing.

Sam Gulino, MD, read the manuscript and made several valuable suggestions for its improvement.

Contents

List of Appendices

List of Figures

Chapter 1
Autopsy Protocol

Purpose, Structure, and Organization

Purpose

The autopsy protocol is the written record of the objective observations made during the examinations conducted by the pathologist. This primary record is often supported by file notes, sketches on body diagrams, and photographs.

A purpose common to all the reports described in this guide is that of answering questions, be they already asked or merely anticipated. Toward this end, reports should be written so as to answer questions, and not so as to raise them unintentionally. Careless use of language can provoke unnecessary questions that must then be answered in deposition or conference months after one's memory of the case has faded.

Autopsy reports are most frequently requested by attorneys, family members, and life insurance companies, and less frequently by clinical physicians. The copies acquired by attorneys are then read by medical experts hired by the attorneys and by in-house medical personnel working for the insurance companies. When constructing a report, the pathologist should be aiming to produce a sound foundation for his or her opinions.

Structure

Objective Versus Subjective

Any report by an expert must clearly separate the objective portions of the report from the subjective parts. The objective part of an autopsy report is customarily known as a *protocol* and consists of findings that would not be disputed by any reasonable pathologist. The autopsy findings do not change with the passage of time. In contrast, the subjective part of an autopsy report consists of the diagnoses, the cause-of-death opinion, and other opinions as needed. The opinions can change if new information is developed from the medical history or circumstances on which the opinions rest.

V.I. Adams, *Guidelines for Reports by Autopsy Pathologists,*
© Humana Press, Totowa, NJ 2008

Protocol Formats

Experienced autopsy pathologists employ a typed narrative format that uses complete sentences to express complete ideas. With this format, sections with important lesions are easily expanded to suit the case, and sections with no important lesions can be executed with brevity. It does take some experience to use this type of format well. This guide is aimed at helping the pathologist produce a professional narrative-style report.

Other formats, usually favored by training programs, employ templates in which the pathologist checks off multiple choices on a preprinted form or fills in the blanks on a preprinted form. Sometimes these forms are converted into a typed report by a secretary or computer software. The advantage is that the novice is less likely to omit an organ or system. The disadvantages are that the report looks like it was generated from boilerplate, and the formats yield much nonessential detail at the expense of essential detail, because every report is treated the same way.

Inadvertent Omission from the Report

One drawback of the narrative format is that an entire organ system can be inadvertently omitted from the dictation. This risk is mitigated by making handwritten notes right after the autopsy. The notes, which need not be extensive, are usually enough to reconstruct a brief description of the undictated organs.

When it is discovered after the body is no longer available that a routine examination has been omitted, or has been done but the findings were omitted from the dictated report, and the handwritten notes are silent, the pathologist should neither invent something plausible nor dictate his or her customary standard wording for unremarkable findings. It is better for the report to be silent than to introduce possibly erroneous information that might become the foundation for an opinion during the course of a deposition months later. An attorney's experts can be in possession of clinical records not originally available to the autopsy pathologist. The attorney in this situation can sometimes know what the autopsy should have shown. The pathologist later asked for an opinion that would depend on the missing observation can decline to offer an opinion, citing any or all of the following possibilities if applicable: (1) The organ was there and was not examined; (2) the organ was there and was examined, but was omitted from the dictated observations; or (3) the organ was not there.

Cut-and-Paste Templates

The use of computer word processing templates permits the pathologist to bypass the professional secretary and construct autopsy reports using cut-and-paste operations. In theory, this is a remarkable labor-saving device. In practice, it has led to professionally embarrassing and seemingly disastrous results, with signed reports describing decomposition in hospital patients, and trauma in decedents who had natural deaths, all as a result of using actual autopsy reports as templates and failing to redact information. Professional secretaries seem to have avoided this problem.

Organization

An autopsy protocol is composed of the following elements, not all of which are used in every case:

1. Inventory of parts
2. Clothing and surface evidence, before cleaning of body
3. External examination (inspection)
4. Findings related to therapeutic devices
5. Findings related to tissue donation
6. Findings related to organ donation
7. Wounds, including external and internal manifestations
8. Internal examination
9. Bone examination for indicia of age, race, sex, stature, wounds, and length of interment
10. Descriptions of fixed organs
11. Microscopic description

Section headers would almost never be used for all of these report elements in one case. For example, a completely skeletonized body would use the inventory, clothing, and bone examination sections. A body dead of natural causes, found at home, might use only the external examination, internal examination, and microscopic description sections.

Measurements

If a lesion is three-dimensional, one can give three-dimensional measurements or a single greatest-dimension measurement. One should not limit the measurements to the two surface dimensions unless the lesion is flat. For any quantitative finding, the report should be written so that the reader can understand whether the number is a measurement or an estimate. A simple way to achieve this end is to dictate the words "an estimated" or "a measured" just before the measurement. The term *approximately* should be avoided; the reader has no way to know if it means a rough measurement or a semiquantitative measurement.

Diagnostic Terms

It is permissible to use a diagnostic term to label a finding within the gross description if one knows that the diagnosis will not be changed by microscopic examination or further history *and* if the lesion is hard to describe. The guiding principle is always: Does it serve the purpose of communication?

However, the report should not use a diagnostic label as a *substitute* for a complete description for any major diagnosis. For example, it is not adequate to state that an organ has decompositional changes; the pathologist must describe what was observed, such as softening, mottling, discoloration, or gas bubbles. And, if one knows that the lung has *pneumonia,* the word can be used. When the pathologist is not sure that the lesion is pneumonia, it is best to merely describe the lesion and reserve the diagnosis for the microscopic section.

On the other hand, a *pneumohemothorax* can be easily and vividly described without using the diagnostic term. In this case, it is better for the report to describe what was seen and felt; namely 300 ml of bloody liquid, and gas under (or not under) tension.

Examples of autopsy protocols are given in Appendices 1 and 2.

External Examination

Inventory of Parts

For remains that have one or more amputations or separate parts, a report that begins with an inventory of parts prevents much confusion on the part of the reader. Examples of such cases can include:

1. Skeletal remains
2. Traumatic amputation
3. Postmortem dismemberment
4. Previous autopsy

Intact Remains

For the vast majority of autopsies, which involve intact and whole remains, the inventory is unstated or implied:

> The body is that of an adult man.

Or, at the end of the external examination:

> The head, neck, torso, and extremities are unremarkable except as indicated.

This sentence completes the external exam not only by indicating that no members are absent by amputation or anomaly, but also by indicating that there is no external sign of disease or wound except as stated and that the entire body has been inspected.

Skeletal Remains

For skeletal remains, the inventory is the central part of the report. It should mention every bone other than those of the hands and feet and state whether each is present or absent. This can be effectively accomplished by one paragraph listing the bones recovered and another paragraph listing the bones not recovered. The hand and foot bones can be described as groups:

> The left hand bones are absent.

Partially Skeletonized Remains

For a decomposed body that is partly skeletonized, the inventory is crucial to writing a clear report. Example:

> The remains consist of a decomposed torso with attached left arm, and separate bones with minimal flesh comprising the skull, the first three cervical vertebrae, the right forearm and hand bones, the left humerus, the left forearm and hand bones, the left and right femurs, tibias, and fibulas, and the right foot bones. The left foot bones are not recovered.

Amputations caused by decomposition can be described in the same section of the report as the signs of decomposition.

Traumatic Amputations

For a body with one or two amputations caused by the trauma of a train or aircraft accident, the inventory is equally important but also quite simple:

> The remains are those of an adult man in four pieces, due to complete amputation of the right leg through the femur and amputation of the 4th and 5th fingers of the left hand.

The full descriptions of these sorts of amputation are usually placed later in the protocol, in the wound descriptions.

Dismemberment to Hide a Body

Similarly, the amputations performed by a person in an effort to hide a homicide, having been mentioned in the inventory, should be described in a separate section constructed for this purpose, and in enough detail to support subsequent conclusions concerning the prospective weapon used for dismemberment.

Previous Autopsy

The protocol for a second autopsy by necessity is longer than that of the original autopsy. A second autopsy is usually demanded because the first autopsy did not answer the reasonably anticipated questions; the report of such a first autopsy is often quite brief. And, the second autopsy protocol is made longer because the usual format is expanded into an inventory, descriptions of fixed organs, the description of the cadaver and any uneviscerated organs, and a description of embalming effect:

Inventory of Body Parts

The remains comprise a cadaver, a plastic bucket with previously dissected organs that have been fixed by embalming, both of which were taken from the disinterred casket; and fixed organs retained until recently by the Pathology Department of Acme Hospital.

Inventory of Fixed Organs

The specimens from the bucket comprise the following, all of which are firm and pink from fixation by embalming compound, some of which adheres to the surfaces:

1. Four horizontal slices of the cardiac ventricles.
2. The base of the heart, previously opened along the flow of blood.

3.   A block comprising the larynx, proximal trachea, hypopharynx, proximal esoph-agus, thyroid gland, and strap muscles. The hypopharynx, esophagus, larynx, and trachea have been previously opened longitudinally from the posterior aspect. The thyroid gland has been previously sectioned at roughly 1-cm intervals perpendicular to the axis of each lobe, through the still-attached strap muscles.

(4., 5., 6., and so forth)

Fixed organs retained by the hospital are limited to the brain, which is completely present except for small samples to be found in the save cup and paraffin blocks. All these specimens are well-fixed:

1.   Eight coronal sections of cerebral hemispheres.
2.   The brainstem and cerebellum, previously sectioned twice through the cerebellum perpendicular to the neural axis, and once through the median sagittal plane of the medulla.

Extent of Previous Autopsy

The cadaver consists of the head, neck, torso, external genitalia, and extremities. It has been previously autopsied by a Y-shaped incision of the anterior aspect of the torso and a coronal incision of the scalp running across the vertex. The skull has a circumferential autopsy cut and lies in place. The dura mater has been previously stripped. The cranial cavity is packed with stained newspaper. The thorax has autopsy cuts through the bony parts of the ribs anteriorly and the medial aspects of the clavicles. The organs of the neck and torso have been previously removed except as noted: The tongue and hyoid bone are in place. The arch of the aorta is absent. The descending aorta has been opened anteriorly but remains attached to the vertebral column. The dome of the urinary bladder has been previously opened; the bladder, seminal vesicles, prostate gland, and testes are otherwise undisturbed. The kidneys have been previously removed; the perinephric fat compartments remain, as do parts of the leaves of the diaphragm.

The autopsy report then takes up with the usual format of external and internal examination and descriptions of wounds.

Clothing and Surface Evidence

Criminal Cases

In criminal cases, the pathologist examines the clothing and searches for surface or trace evidence before the body is cleaned, and records the findings in the scene report, in the autopsy, or both, depending on where the search was conducted. A pathologist who goes to the scene and makes the examination of clothing part of the scene report does not need to re-inventory the clothing as part of the autopsy report. But if the clothing came in with the body, the autopsy report should at least state that the clothing is not further remarkable.

Noncriminal Cases

For natural deaths, most accidental deaths, and most suicidal deaths, the as-is pho-tographs and written inventories compiled by the morgue technician usually consti-tute sufficient documentation of the clothing and no description of the clothing by the pathologist is required.

Identifying Features

For bodies that are free of trauma, tattoos, scars, and therapeutic devices and have not undergone tissue donation, the external examination is usually a brief description of unremarkable anatomical regions and identifying features. These two aspects are usually combined in a single paragraph.

Age, Length, and Weight

The report should include an estimate of age and the measured length and weight of the body. If the pathologist has not personally weighed and measured the body but these measurements were made and appear in a header at the top or front of the autopsy report, it is sufficient to state that the body appears consistent with the stated age, length, and weight. If the body appears older than the listed age, this should be stated. If the body appears heavier, lighter, longer, or shorter than the listed values, new measurements should be made and incorporated into the description.

Identifying Features

In this section are features that are sometimes useful for helping to exclude or confirm identity. This section is also a convenient repository for the routine mention of unremarkable limbs and orifices, including the mouth, genitalia, and anus. The section should include sex, body build, skin tone, color and texture of scalp hair, facial hair, dentition, female breasts, genitalia, anus, scars, distinctive moles, old amputations, and tattoos.

The description of racial features may be a simple label or a description of skin and hair characteristics. With respect to such simple labels, *Hispanic* is not a race; the term refers to Spanish-language use or ancestry and was popularized by the U.S. Census Bureau.

When the description of the body refers to the decedent (as is the case when one writes "the body is that of a 55-year-old woman"), one should use the humanizing term *woman* or *girl* rather than *female*, and *man* or *boy* rather than *male*. The reason for this is to indicate in at least one place that the body is that of a human and not that of some other species. However, *adolescent male* and *adolescent female* are acceptable for adolescents.

The report should describe *body build* in simple terms, for example, *medium build, lean, emaciated, cachectic, large-boned, muscular, obese*, and the like. If the body is emaciated, the report should include some supporting descriptions, such as prominent ribs and hollow temples. If the body is markedly obese, the report should describe whether the extra adipose tissue is concentrated in a few areas such as the abdomen or is distributed proportionately over the torso and limbs. In the morbidly obese, it is useful to convey some idea of impaired respiratory mechanics by describing thick chest walls or a neck that is short and encased in fat. If apparently high body weight is caused by large muscle mass or a large frame (large-caliber bones), one should say so. Avoid the term *overweight*; it implies that one is comparing the body weight to some ideal or standard weight. Better to describe what is seen:

The body is that of an adult woman appearing the above-stated length and weight and appearing older than the stated age. Body build is medium but extremely obese; the extra adipose deposits involve the torso, hips, thighs, axillae, and neck. The chest walls are extraordinarily thickened by fat. The neck is short and encased in fat; the shoulders are at the level of the chin.

Eyes

The examination of the eyes should include at a minimum the iris color and the presence or absence of conjunctival petechiae.

Scalp Hair

The report should include the color and texture of any scalp hair. The texture can be described as straight, wavy, curly, or tightly curled; and thick or thin. Because the meaning of *short*, *medium*, and *long* depends on the prevailing fashion at the time the report is made, the preferred mode of description is an estimate of the hair length in centimeters or inches. An actual measurement is not necessary. For men, the distribution of the scalp hair can be indicated as full, or with bifrontal balding, frontal balding, or vertex balding.

Scalp hair is gray, curly, thin, and an estimated 4 inches long. The frontal and vertex regions of the scalp are nearly bald.

Facial Hair

Facial hair can be any combination of the following: moustache, imperial (hair on the lower lip), goatee, sideburns, wispy adolescent facial hair, and untrimmed stubble.

Dentition

If present, dentition can be mentioned as being in good, fair, or poor repair. If dentition is not present, the report should indicate whether the mouth is edentulous or, in the case of a baby, that the mouth has no erupted teeth. The description should mention whether any bridges or full plates are in the mouth. This can be important if the funeral director later calls looking for such items.

Scars

The report should always mention scars even if only to state that there are no apparent surgical scars. Scars need not be measured unless the identity of the body is unknown. Otherwise, the characterization of a scar as small, medium, or large, with respect to the anatomical region in which the scar is found, is sufficient. Scars are old and healed by definition unless otherwise described; therefore, a scar does not need to be described as old and well healed unless a particular investigational point is being addressed. However, a healing wound can be partly scarred. If the pathologist recognizes a specific type of scar such as a thoracotomy scar or a vaccination scar, that specific designation can be used in the report. Otherwise, a scar can be described as linear, round, oval, irregular, flat, raised, and the like. A separate paragraph for scars is useful if the scars are numerous. Because scars can suggest prior surgery or suicide attempts, they are sometimes helpful in identifying a body.

Amputations

Mention all amputations. However, amputated foreskin is customarily reported as circumcision of the male genitalia.

Tattoos

Every external examination should mention tattoos, if only to say there are none. In the case of unidentified remains, the tattoos should be not only described but also photographed so that the photos can be used for the purpose of identification. If identification is not an issue, multiple tattoos can be described in a brief summary sentence without describing individual tattoos.

> The upper back region has a large, professionally executed polychrome tattoo depicting an eagle.

Or:

> The torso, neck, and extremities have multiple polychrome tattoos featuring frequent skulls.

Or:

> The fingers, hands, and forearms have several amateur-quality gray-tone tattoos.

Identifying Tags and Bracelets

It is not useful to describe the toe tags placed by one's own employees in the autopsy suite. However, it can be useful to describe hospital identification bracelets. Toe tags placed by hospital personnel on a dead body are of less interest because one has no assurance that such tags were placed by personnel who knew the decedent.

> The left wrist has a hospital identification bracelet bearing the decedent's name.

Lesions: Disease and Minor Wounds

The remainder of the external examination is concerned with describing lesions caused by disease or injury. If there are no injuries, one can say so. If there are wounds but they are few and trivial, they can be described in the same paragraph with the identifying features.

Pitfalls

Identifying features constitute the part of the autopsy report that the next-of-kin are competent to evaluate. A correct description of identifying features suggests to family members that the report is thorough and that the body is really that of their loved one. Both carelessness as well as thoroughness in the description of such features may lead the kin to doubt the parts of the report that they are not competent to evaluate. For example, under full-spectrum lighting, the pathologist may decide that the eyes are gray, but for the family it is an established fact that the eyes are blue. Or, the report mentions faint linear scars on the knee that the family knows to be from cat scratches 40 years prior, but the family finds no mention of the almost invisible scar on the chin from a fall in childhood. In anticipation of these sorts of difficulties, the pathologist may well opt to describe the irides as being of an indeterminate color and to state that the body has no *apparent surgical* scars.

Signs of Death

If the signs of death have been described in a scene report, there is no compelling reason to use the autopsy report to describe the effects of subsequent refrigeration. However, the pathologist who makes it a routine to include signs of death in the autopsy is less likely to forget their mention in a scene report. For this reason, the author's office requires the inclusion of a description of the signs of death in all autopsy reports.

Livor Mortis

The report should describe the color of the livor, state whether the postmortem hypostasis is fixed, unfixed, or partially fixed, and remark whether it is anterior, posterior, or in some other aspect of the remains. The degree of lividity should be described. For the typical posterior lividity pattern of a supine, stored body, the extent can be described as rising to the any of the vertical anatomical lines of the torso, such as the posterior, middle, and anterior axillary lines; and the level of the nipples. If the lividity is intense enough to produce Tardieu spots, these should be mentioned. A description of facial livor can be helpful when a family later wonders if the face was bruised.

Rigor Mortis

A frequent and useless practice of the novice pathologist is to state whether rigor is strong or weak. The perceived strength of rigor mortis simply reflects the muscle mass of the dead body relative to that of the pathologist. Rigor mortis should be graded as absent, oncoming, fully developed, or passing. It can be useful to describe where the rigor was tested, such as the jaw.

Algor Mortis

In warm climates, it is sufficient to state whether the body is warm, cool, or cold to palpation. It can be helpful to add "from refrigeration" for stored bodies. For scene reports in cool climates, thermometer readings of rectal or liver temperature may well be helpful. In the author's practice location of Florida, thermometer readings are helpful only for diagnosing hyperthermia.

Drying Artifact

The red-brown drying artifact of the eyes, *tache noire*, should not be described as lividity. The scrotum sometimes appears abraded for no good reason, possibly from drying alone.

Putrefaction

The report should describe putrid odors, bloating, skin slippage, drying change, marbling, discoloration of lividity, fly eggs, maggots, and defects of flesh caused by maggots in detail sufficient for the purposes of the autopsy. In a death by natural causes, the description can be brief. In a homicide, it is helpful to mention putrefactive changes that might be taken for wounds in a photograph. Lividity of the face, especially if it has undergone putrefactive darkening, can be taken for bruising by family members or funeral directors and for this reason is useful to include in the description.
Scene:

Rigor mortis is oncoming in the jaw and barely apparent elsewhere. The torso is warm to touch. Faint blanchable pink dependent lividity consistent with the position of the body has begun to form.

Autopsy:

Rigor mortis is fully developed. The torso is cold from refrigeration. Livor mortis is posterior, unfixed, and rises to the mid-axillary lines.

Or:

The body is in the early stages of putrefactive decomposition as manifested by several areas of skin slippage, dark green marbling of areas of dependent livor especially around the face and neck, gaseous distension of the abdomen, fly eggs on the eyes, and a faint putrid odor.

Embalmed Bodies

For a body that has been embalmed, the description of embalming effects can replace the usual description of signs of death. One should describe the location of embalmer's incisions, their sutures, the location of trocar holes externally and internally, the extent of fixation externally and internally, any artifactual effusions in body cavities, the contents of vessels and cardiac chambers, and odor.

The body has been embalmed by arterial perfusion and by trocar. The right subclavian region has an embalmer's incision closed with twine. The nearby subclavian muscle has been divided and is coated with drying compound. A trocar button fills a trocar hole in the right upper quadrant of the abdominal wall. The skin is somewhat firm from fixation. The posterior surfaces of the torso have minimal residual lividity. The eyes are covered with plastic embalmer's caps. The jaws are tied shut with embalmer's twine.

The mesentery, liver, and loops of intestine have multiple trocar holes, all about 1 cm in diameter. The diaphragmatic leaves, lungs, and heart have a few trocar holes. The tissue surrounding these defects is firm, gray, and well fixed. The peritoneal cavity has an estimated 200 ml of turbid gray-brown liquid with a few pieces of feces. The pleural cavities each have an estimated 100 ml of nearly clear tan liquid.

The chambers of the heart and the great vessels are filled with a mixture of firm, fixed, red-brown clots and thin red-brown liquid with an odor of formalin.

Organization of External Findings

In offices where the external examination is dictated contemporaneously with the examination, the report is usually organized by body region. This can produce a cluttered, hard-to-read format. Dictating after the autopsy from notes made on diagrams permits the report to be organized with separate paragraphs for therapy, tissue donation, organ donation, and wounds.

Therapy

A separate paragraph with its own header to set off the descriptions of therapeutic devices is useful because the reader of the protocol is usually scanning to answer a particular question and is either interested in the device placement or not. If not interested, the reader sees the descriptions of medical devices as visual clutter. In either case, the placement of these descriptions in a separate paragraph serves the purpose of clarity.

Cardiac Electrodes

If the paramedics put the leads on for the sole purpose of establishing that death occurred and not for therapeutic purposes, and the leads are the only medical devices, the report does not need a separate therapy section. Unless electrodes cover wounds or other lesions of interest, it is sufficient to locate the electrodes as being on the torso or extremities.

Tubes and Catheters

The principal purpose of describing a tube or catheter is to state whether the device is in the proper passage. One should describe the entry site and the termination site.

Surgical Repairs

Internal surgical repairs and artifacts can be described in the section for wounds, in the therapy section, or in the internal examination, depending on what makes the best sense for the individual case.

Unneeded Information

The dates written on devices and bandages by hospital personnel might be of later interest to a malpractice attorney, but are usually of little concern if the autopsy is performed in the public interest by a medical examiner. If such information is of interest, the simplest way to capture it is by photography rather than by copying it onto diagrams and dictating it into the report.

Therapy:

An orotracheal tube, previously cut flush with the face, runs from the mouth to the trachea. Intravenous catheters are in the left antecubital fossa and the right groin. A right subclavian catheter passes through the right chambers of the heart and ends in the pulmonary artery. The torso has multiple cardiac electrodes. The skin over the sternum has an abraded contusion (Comment: chest compressions). A hospital identification bracelet on the left wrist is labeled Trauma T123; another on the right wrist is labeled with the decedent's name.

Organ and Tissue Donation

Postmortem Tissue Donation

If a body undergoes postmortem donation of skin, bones, or eyes before the internal examination, the external examination should includes a paragraph for observations concerning eye changes; the distribution of bone donation incisions, sutures, and skin donor sites; and other changes in the condition of the returned body such as reduction in the prominence of livor mortis. The paragraph should describe only what is seen by the pathologist. For example, it would mention the sutured donation wounds on the extremities, but would not speculate about which bones were removed unless the wounds were opened for inspection.

The report should clearly indicate whether the external examination of such a body occurred before or after tissue donation. This can be accomplished by including the date and time for each examination. If external examinations are done both before and after tissue donation, the second examination can be limited to the signs of donation.

The body having been returned from the tissue bank is re-examined on 11 May at 1030 hrs: The lower extremities have sutured wounds corresponding to long-bone retrieval. The back and lower extremities have multiple large, somewhat rectangular, pink abrasion-like areas corresponding to skin retrieval. The corneas have been excised.

Vascular Organ Donation

Similarly, for cases of vascular organ donation, a separate paragraph is useful to list not only the organs that were removed for transplantation, but also the tissue removed incidental to organ removal, such as the aorta, adrenal glands, and perinephric fat; surgical defects in the diaphragm and pericardial sac; bloody fluid in the resulting common cavity; and surgical mobilization of bowel.

> The torso has a vertically oriented recent incised wound running from the manubrial area to the pubis. It is sutured closed. The sternum has a recent sternotomy. The heart, liver, and kidneys are absent due to recent vascular organ retrieval, along with the aortic arch, the adrenals glands, a portion of the spleen, the perinephric fat, the abdominal aorta, the inferior vena cava, and the perilumbar retroperitoneal fat and lymph nodes. The diaphragmatic leaves and the pericardial sac have multiple surgical incisions, creating a common body cavity, in which is an estimated 200 ml of thin, pink liquid. The large and small intestines have been surgically mobilized.

Wounds by Type

General Organization

Sections of the Report

A separate section with its own header for wounds is warranted whenever the manner of death is unnatural or, in the case of natural deaths, when the description of wounds takes up more than a few lines. This section can be a simple list of external wound descriptions or, for major trauma cases, a highly organized list of descriptions of external and internal wounds with headers for blunt impact wounds by body regions (head and neck, torso, extremities, for example), gunshot wounds, blade wounds, burns, and other wounds.

Pertinent Negatives

Formatting with a separate wound section works better if one does not insert pertinent negatives in the wound section, because they tend to clutter the section. Pertinent negatives work best in the internal examination section.

From the wound section of the report:

1. The base of the skull has a complete transverse fracture running through the roofs of the middle ears and the body of the sphenoid bone.The overlying dura mater is torn over the left petrous ridge.
2. The brain has small, faint cerebrocortical contusions and thin, patchy subarachnoid hemorrhages of the inferior aspects of the temporal lobes in relation to the above-described basilar fracture.

Same report, from the internal examination:

> *Head.* The scalp, skull, and meninges are remarkable as indicated. The epidural and subdural spaces have no blood. The brain weights 1290 grams. The cranial nerves and cerebral arteries are unremarkable. The brain is not swollen. The brainstem has no lacerations. The white matter has no hemorrhages. The external and cut surfaces of the brain are remarkable only as indicated.

Outside-In

For each region of the body, the report is organized to begin with cutaneous wounds, followed by skeletal wounds, and then visceral wounds.

When beginning a new region, the first paragraph typically describes skin wounds. It is useful to insert the word *skin* or *cutaneous* in the first paragraph of a new section to help the reader know that the narrative has left the internal organs of the preceding body region and has returned to the integument. An immediately following paragraph that deals with skin wounds need not repeat *skin* or *cutaneous*.

WOUNDS: EXTERNAL AND INTERNAL
Torso

(Preceding paragraphs omitted)
The pelvis has a laceration of the symphysis pubis joint with 6 cm of distraction. The urogenital diaphragm and the anterior aspect of the urinary bladder are lacerated, permitting communication between the lumen of the bladder and the peritoneal cavity. An estimated 100 ml of extravasated blood is in the pelvic sidewall tissue.
Extremities

The left upper extremity has large cutaneous tan- red abrasions of the dorsal aspect of the forearm and hand.

Paragraphs

Clarity

For wound descriptions, the text should be broken up into paragraphs that are as short as possible to make them easier to scan and read. For the internal descriptions of impact wounds, separate paragraphs for each organ are preferred. For instance, separate paragraphs for the skull, dura, and brain help to achieve clarity.

Numbering

Placing Arabic numerals in front of each paragraph in the wound section allows for easy reference during conferences and depositions and gives the text of this section an appearance distinctive from the external and internal examination sections. This can be useful when flipping open a report to gain rapid orientation to the layout of the report.

Summary Paragraphs

For complicated protocols with many wounds, summary paragraphs with the subtotals of the numbers of wounds are helpful. Attorneys like to count wounds. Such summary paragraphs are placed above the descriptive paragraphs.

WOUND SUMMARY
The body has multiple stab, incised, and blunt impact wounds.
Fourteen stab wounds are located as follows: neck (1), torso (9), right upper extremity (1),

left upper extremity (1), left lower extremity (2).
Four incised wounds are located as follows: neck (3), right upper extremity (1).
Ten blunt impact wounds are located as follows: head (2), left upper extremity (5), right upper extremity (3).
The wound descriptions follow.
STAB AND INCISED WOUNDS
Stab Wound to Neck

The right side of the neck has a stab wound centered 54" above the outstep of the right foot and 1" to the right of the median sagittal plane.

See Appendices 1 and 2 for examples of autopsy protocols with sections for wounds.

Impact Wounds

Description

For cutaneous wounds, the description of an abrasion, contusion, or laceration should indicate what part of the body is involved.

The right pectoral region of the chest has a small red abrasion.

A description of a laceration should indicate the nature of the tissue that is penetrated by a laceration.

The left parietal region of the scalp has a 4 × 2 cm laceration that penetrates through the galea to the skull.
The right thigh anteriorly has a 10 × 3 × 3 cm laceration that penetrates to the investing fascia.

The terms *abrasion* rather than *scrape, contusion* rather than *bruise*, and *laceration* rather than *tear* are preferred in the interest of producing a professional-appearing report.

Size

For traffic accidents, one can measure abrasions and contusions if they are patterned, and otherwise state only that they are small, medium, or large. Photographs and diagrams record the shape and distribution of abrasions and contusions better than the narrative descriptions. In warm climates where the clothing is light, the victims of traffic crashes tend to have a multitude of nonpatterned skin wounds, the measurement of which adds nothing of significance to the report.

The posterior aspect of the right thigh has a rectangular 10 × 14 cm patterned wound. This wound comprises two vertically oriented, parallel 10 × 1 cm red abrasions, between which are multiple areas of pink dermal contusions.
    The left forearm has a large, dry, tan abrasion dorsally. The dorsal aspect of the left hand has multiple small tan abrasions.

However, for lacerations, measurements should be given in three dimensions: two on the surface, and one for the depth (example above). And, in the case of a homicide, *all* wounds should be measured, including nonpatterned abrasions and contusions.

Acute, Chronic, or Postmortem

The description should be explicit as to whether the wound is acute or healing. If the description is not explicit, the reader should be able to infer whether the wound is acute or healing from the context.

> The left side of the forehead has a 2 × 1 cm moist, red abrasion. [Inference: acute pre-mortem, or postmortem in area of dependent lividity]
>
> The left side of the forehead has a 2 × 1 cm dry, tan, parchment-like abrasion. [Inference: peri- or postmortem]

Scabs can form on lesions other than wounds, such as blisters and pustules. If the scabs are on healing wounds, one can list them with the other wounds. If they are probably nontraumatic lesions, they can be placed in the regular part of the external examination.

> The lateral aspect of the right side of the thorax has a 1.5 cm dry, round, red excoriation with subtle scarring of the adjacent skin (Comment: wound vs. benign medical lesion).

If one thinks a wound was incurred when the decedent collapsed dead, a parenthetical comment can be inserted to convey this opinion.

> The left eyebrow has a 2 × 0.3 × 0.2 cm blood- lined laceration of the skin (Comment: dead-fall wound).

Blade Wounds

Location

A stab wound or incised wound should be located in two ways. It should be assigned to a named body region such as the pectoral region of the chest or the temple region of the head. And, distances to fixed landmarks should be employed to help locate the wound. Because it is not used for ballistic reconstruction, the distance of a stab wound of the chest from the sole of a foot is not important. Recording the distance from the anterior or posterior midline of the torso is useful.

> The left upper quadrant of the abdomen has a stab wound centered 4 cm from the anterior midline.

Unless otherwise stated, the distance of the wound from another point is taken to mean the distance from the center of the wound.

Description

The report should state the length and width of a wound at the skin surface and the orientation of the wound at the surface. For example:

> The wound is 5 × 2 × 0.3 cm and oriented obliquely with the lateral end uppermost.

Use of an imaginary clock face axis conveys the orientation more precisely:

> The wound is 5 × 2 × 0.3 cm and oriented from 8 to 2 o'clock.

For a stab wound, an attempt should be made to classify the ends of the surface wound as pointed or blunt.

Depth

The depth of wound may be estimated, approximated, or measured, depending on the wound path, but some number should be given.

The difficulty in stating a precise depth is illustrated by a stab wound that penetrates the abdominal cavity. Once the blade passes through the abdominal wall, it may penetrate several centimeters into the cavity without encountering a loop of bowel. Or it may penetrate several loops of bowels, but because loops of bowel are mobile, the observed location of the bowel wounds with respect to the abdominal wall may bear little relation to the location of the loops at the time the blade was inserted. For such an abdominal wound, the estimate of depth may have to be limited to the thickness of the abdominal wall.

A better approximation can be had with a wound to the chest that penetrates the heart. In this case, one can measure the static (as the body lies) depth of the wound from the skin surface, as say, 7 cm. Later, in testimony, one can explain that the dynamic wound path may have been longer, due to full inspiratory expansion of the chest, or smaller, due to compression of the chest by the hilt of the knife.

Path

The path of the wound should be stated in terms of the organs and tissues penetrated, and the end of the path should be located. The report should state the direction of path with respect to standard anatomical position, and for tangential wounds, the direction of path with respect to the surface of the body. For wounds that approach but do not penetrate body cavities, one should state that there is no penetration of the cavity.

Associated Findings

Associated findings, such as blood in cavities and soft tissue, or foreign material in the wound, should be described.

Stab Wound of Chest

The left side of the chest has a stab wound in the pectoral region 1/2 inch superior to the nipple and 3 inches to the left of the anterior midline. The skin perforation is 3.0×1.2 cm and is oriented obliquely with the superior end lateral. The superior end of the wound is blunt and the inferior end is sharp. With approximation of the edges, the wound is 3.2 cm long.

The wound path penetrates the pectoralis muscles, the cartilage of the left 3rd rib, and the 3rd intercostal space and enters the left pleural cavity as a 2.9-cm-long defect of the parietal pleura. The path then runs through the lingula of the left lung and ends by nicking the left side of the pericardial sac without perforation.

The wound depth from skin surface to pericardial sac is estimated at 3 inches.

The direction of the wound path with respect to the standard anatomical position is back, to the right, and slightly down.

The left pleural cavity has a measured 1400 ml of dark red blood that is partly clotted, and a small quantity of gas not under tension.

Hanging

For suicidal hanging deaths with no significant drop, the wound description comprises the ligature and the cutaneous ligature mark, and any fractures of the hyoid bone or laryngeal cartilages. It is helpful to use two paragraphs, one for the ligature and one for the mark and any internal findings.

Ligature

If one has some knowledge of knot-making, it can be used to describe the knots. Otherwise, one can simply indicate whether the knot is a slip knot or a non-slip knot. The material employed as a noose should be described, and its width should be given. For example:

> A 1/4-inch white nylon sash cord with a woven pattern.
> A 3/8-inch orange heavy-duty electrical extension cord with a smooth surface.

Ligature Mark

The report should state whether the ligature mark has patterned imprints corresponding to the ligature. The description should include a suspension point, even if it is not imprinted and is merely inferred by the slope of the ligature mark on other parts of the neck. As an adjunct to the statement of the suspension point, one can measure the distance from each earlobe to the ligature mark, to objectively convey the symmetry or asymmetry of the ligature mark.

The description should include the width and depth of the ligature mark and enough description to convey some sense of its appearance. For instance, a recent ligature mark might be a simple, blanched, unfurrowed stripe with intense adjacent nonblanching lividity. Or, the mark might be a tan furrow due to compressive desiccation of the skin and the underlying subcutaneous tissue. The report should include any focal abrasions in or along the furrow, as these might correspond to slippage of the noose, or to manual attempts by the decedent to adjust the noose.

An objective way to convey the degree of constriction is to measure the respective circumferences of the ligature and the neck. When the circumference of the ligature is, for example, 2 inches less than that of the neck, it creates a compelling mental image for the reader of the report.

The internal examination centers on the search for fractures of the hyoid bone and laryngeal cartilages. If found, the degree of blood extravasation should be stated, as these wounds can occur postmortem from prolonged suspension.

> The neck has a ligature mark corresponding to the ligature just described. Anteriorly it runs just superior to the laryngeal prominence. It ascends on each side of the neck such that it lies 5 cm inferior to the left earlobe and 7 cm inferior to the right earlobe. It is a tan, dry furrow with an imprint matching the weave of the ligature. Anteriorly the mark is 0.6 cm wide and 0.7 cm deep. On each side of the neck it gradually widens to 1.0 cm and becomes shallower. The mark peters out on the posterior aspect of the neck, where

the left and right elements of the mark point to a suspension point near the left side of the occipital protuberance. The superior margin of the ligature mark just to the left of the anterior midline has a 1.5×0.3 cm red-tan abrasion. The skin superior to the ligature mark is more congested than below. The subcutaneous tissue beneath the mark is compressed and desiccated.

Firearm Wounds

A convenient way to organize the description of a gunshot wound or a shotgun wound is to have separate paragraphs for the following:

1. Entrance perforation
2. Path (Sequence of tissues perforated)
3. Exit perforation OR bullet
4. Direction of travel with respect to anatomical position
5. Associated findings

Entrance Perforation

The report should locate the wound in a body region and give distances to anatomical landmarks in feet and inches. The most useful landmarks are the outstep of the foot and the anterior or posterior midline of the torso. Although the distances to landmarks are best given in inches for the convenience of scene reconstruction, wound measurements in the English system are cumbersome because of the fractions required.

> The entrance perforation is on the left buttock, 31" superior to the out-step of the left foot and 4" to the left of the posterior midline.

The practice of using the top of the shoulder as a reference point is not recommended, because the shoulder slopes and is movable. The top of the head is a better reference but is inferior to the sole of the foot for two reasons: (1) The top of the head is round, so the plane of the top of the head is difficult to define; and (2) because trigonometric ballistic reconstruction works from the ground level, the reconstructionist will use the top-of-head measurement coupled with the body length to *derive* a wound-to-sole distance. If the length of the body is determined by a morgue technician, the pathologist cannot testify to its correctness. A calculated measurement based on two measured numbers is inherently less accurate than a single measured number.

For suicidal trans-temporal gunshot wounds of the head, it is sufficient to employ the distance superior or inferior to, and anterior or posterior to, the upper ear attachment.

> The entrance wound is at the right temple region of the head, anterior to the hairline, 4 cm anterior to the upper ear attachment and 1 cm superior to this point.
> The exit perforation is at the left temple, in the hair-bearing region of the scalp, 2 cm posterior to the upper ear attachment and 1 cm superior to this point.

Abrasion Collar and Perforation

One should describe the abrasion collar as regular or irregular. An irregular shape can suggest an intermediate target. The location of maximum width of the abrasion collar is conveniently given by the use of clock face numbers. Either centimeters or millimeters can be used for the wound measurements. Using millimeters removes the need for decimal points.

There are two ways to measure the abrasion collar and the perforation. The preferred method is to give the diameter of the wound, including both the collar and the perforation, and then the diameter of the enclosed perforation, and to indicate where the collar is widest. This method is preferred because the outline of the abrasion more closely matches the outline of the impacting bullet than does the outline of the perforation.

> The wound, including the abrasion collar, is round and 14 mm in diameter. It encloses a 9-mm round perforation. The abrasion collar is widest at the 2 o'clock position.

The alternative method is to measure the perforation diameter and state the range of widths of the abrasion collar, indicating where it is widest.

> The perforation is round and 9 mm in diameter. The adjacent epidermis has a marginal abrasion extending from the 11 to 5 o'clock positions and has a maximum width of 3 mm at the 2 o'clock position.

If a muzzle stamp is present, it should be described and measured. If there is none, this should be stated.

Fouling

One should measure the extent of soot deposition or state if soot is absent from the skin adjacent to the wound.

> Soot on the adjacent skin extends up to 4 cm from the center of the wound.

Stippling should be described as having a dense, medium, or sparse distribution. One should give a diameter of the stippled zone if it is radially symmetric, and if not, several radial distances to the perforation.

> Sparse gunpowder stippling involves the skin around the wound, extending 10 cm superiorly, 6 cm to the left, 6 cm inferiorly, and 4 cm to the right.

The report should note the presence of any residual flakes of gunpowder in the stippled lesions. Such flakes are commonly observed at the scene before the body is disturbed, and uncommonly at autopsy.

Path

This paragraph describes the internal wounds. At a minimum, it is a simple, sequential recitation of the organs, cavities, and tissue penetrated by the bullet or shot, ending with a brief reference to the exit location and a statement that there is no bullet, or a statement that the path ends in a particular location.

A more elegant construction is to use two paragraphs, the first with the minimal list of organs for laymen, and the second, giving more anatomical detail, for physicians. When bone is penetrated and there is no exit wound, one should indicate the direction of body splinters as an adjunct to determining the direction of fire. Example:

> The wound path runs through the scalp, temporalis muscle, skull, brain, and ends in the right side of the skull in the temporal region. The wound path is described in the following detail:
>
> The entrance perforation of the skull involves the left frontal bone and is internally beveled. It continues through the dura and enters the brain, where the path involves the left parietal lobe, the left lateral ventricle, the basal ganglia, and the right temporal lobe. The path continues through the dura on the right and ends in an externally beveled comminuted fracture in the right temporal region of the skull.

Terminology

The description will read more clearly if the verbs *perforate* and *penetrate* are used rather than *lacerate*. By convention, forensic pathologists avoid the term *laceration* when describing gunshot wounds, to preclude confusion with blunt impact trauma. *Perforate* means "through." *Penetrate* means that the bullet enters but does not exit.

Exit Perforation

The location of the exit perforation, if there is one, should be referenced to fixed anatomical landmarks as described above and should also be referenced to a named anatomical region.

The description should have sufficient detail to permit an informed reader to reliably distinguish between entrance and exit perforations. This is especially important if the exit wound has an abrasion collar. Abrasion collars for simple entrance wounds are usually regular, either round or crescentic. Collars for shored exit perforations and for entrance perforations that follow intermediate targets are usually irregular in shape.

The description should mention the presence or absence of a tissue deficit if it can be ascertained. Entrances seem to have a deficit and exit wounds seem to have no tissue deficit.

If there is no bullet in the body, the report should so state. One should avoid a statement such as, "The projectile is not recovered from the end of the wound track." This sentence can be variously interpreted to mean (1) there was a bullet, but it was not in the body, (2) there was a bullet in the wound track, but it was not at the end of the wound track, or (3) there was a bullet at the end of the wound track, but the pathologist chose not to retrieve it.

Bullet

The paragraph for the projectile must state the location where the bullet or shot is found. This is usually the end of the wound path and can be so stated. Although the pathologist should not introduce actual measurements of the projectile that might later conflict with those produced by the firearms examiner, it is useful and common to give a rough estimate of caliber as small, medium, or large. If a bullet is jacketed, this should be stated, along with an indication of whether the jacket is copper, steel, or another metal. If the bullet and its jacket are separate, the report should describe their locations and their separate paths. One should describe the degree of deformation and marring of the bullet and its jacket. The report should include any inscription made on the base of the bullet. If the bullet is photographed, this can be stated, along with a remark that it is photographed on its labeled evidence envelope prior to being sealed in the envelope.

> Recovered from the end of the wound path is a medium-caliber unjacketed lead bullet with mild deformation. It is left uninscribed and is photographed on its labeled evidence envelope before being sealed in the envelope.

Trajectory

With reference to the standard anatomical position, the report should indicate whether the bullet went from front to back, left to right, up or down. The clearest construction is to give the major component first. Measuring angles with respect to an imaginary anatomical plane does not add anything worthwhile, because the body can bend.

> The direction of the wound path, with respect to the standard anatomical position, is front to back, to the left, and slightly down.

Associated Findings

Other findings are placed in a paragraph for associated findings. Here the report describes volumes of blood in body cavities, radiating skull fractures, venous air embolisms, stippling from the cylinder gap, and anything else that does not fit in one of the categories above. This paragraph often contains the information of interest to clinical physicians.

Burns and Fire Deaths

Percentage of Body Surface

Usually, the easiest way to ascertain the percentage of the skin surface that is burned is to use the assessment done by the burn surgeon. There is no point in introducing a different number if the assessment at the hospital is reasonable. If the decedent did not go to the hospital, an exact percentage is not needed; these victims either have primary smoke inhalation and acquire postmortem burns after a fire spreads or have charring involving most of the body.

Description

It is not sufficient to simply state that a burn is of the second or third degree. One must also describe the burns. The basic discriminators for burn descriptions at autopsy are as follows: Fourth degree burns are charred or calcined. Generally, these burns are described without using the term *fourth degree*. With third-degree burns, the dermis is hard, not supple. In second-degree burns, the epidermis is blistered off. First-degree burns cannot be determined in a dead body because they are manifested by vasogenic erythema, which is a vital phenomenon. In addition to these basics, one adds color, moistness, and therapy such as grafts and graft donation sites.

Fractures and Lacerations

If the pathologist determines that a fracture is heat-induced, that opinion can be introduced directly in the protocol if there is no doubt about the opinion. If calvarial fractures are visible on external examination, the report should say so, to preclude a reader from thinking that they were visible only on internal inspection.

Airways

For any burn victim, the report should state whether the upper airways and bronchi have soot. In those fire victims who are primarily overcome by smoke, the report should describe any red livor of the viscera.

Treatment

The wounds of a burn victim who survives for any length of time in a hospital are considerably altered by treatment. Burned necrotic tissue is commonly debrided, leaving a base of unburned, raw tissue to be covered by grafts. The report should describe any skin grafts, with the extent and location of coverage, and whether the grafts are adherent. Skin donor sites should be briefly described. Surgeons have a choice of several types of grafts; the hospital record should be consulted to avoid mislabeling the grafts.

Wounds by Organ

Measurements

Measurement of Lacerations

The measurements of major lacerations should be given in three dimensions. The depth of a laceration can be given descriptively if that is more informative:

> The scalp has a curvilinear 5 × 4 cm laceration involving the full thickness of the scalp.

Versus:

> The scalp has a curvilinear 5 × 4 × 0.7 cm laceration that penetrates to the galea aponeurotica.

Other lacerations can be sized with one measurement for the greatest dimension:

> A 1 cm in-greatest-dimension laceration.

Measurement of Blood Extravasations

Hematomas in soft tissue that cannot be volumetrically measured, as in fasciae and connective tissue, should be estimated, to enable subsequent calculations of percentage of blood volume lost. Example:

> The pelvic sidewall tissues have an estimated 100 ml of extravasated blood.

Bones: General

A fracture is simply a laceration of a crystalline tissue. Thus, bones fracture and intervertebral discs lacerate. The pathologist should therefore describe a joint derangement as a laceration unless the joint is fused by ankylosis or the derangement includes a fracture of one of the adjacent bones. Surgeons often use the term *fracture* loosely to include lacerations of the liver and kidneys, which, together with bones, seem to have the common physical property of having tissue that is too dense to develop a visible contusion.

Most fractures can be described as complete or incomplete. A complete fracture extends across the entire width of the bone. Some skull fractures are limited to the outer table; some rib fractures are only cracks of the outer cortex.

The distinction is important because a complete fracture can be dislocated or distracted. A dislocated fracture has a much higher risk of tearing soft tissue than a fracture that has not dislocated. The report of a fracture of a long bone or rib should include whether the fracture is dislocated and, at least by implication, whether adjacent soft tissue is lacerated. The absence of static dislocation does not preclude there having been dynamic dislocation at the time of impact. Not surprisingly, complete fractures with no static dislocation can be associated with soft tissue lacerations.

The description of a fracture should include an estimate of the volume of blood extravasated into adjacent soft tissue.

Skull and Dura

One should describe fractures of the skull in terms of the structures they traverse, including as locators the fossae, foramina, and ridges of the base of the skull, the roofs of the middle ears, and the dural sinuses.

Whenever a skull fracture is described, the report should also indicate whether the corresponding region of dura mater is intact, loosened, or torn. Tearing of the dura in general requires more force than fracturing the skull; the presence of a dural laceration is often indicative of an impact sufficiently severe as to cause immediate lethal concussion.

> The base of the skull has a complete transverse fracture that involves the roofs of the middle ears and the body of the sphenoid bone. It has no static dislocation. The dura over the left cavernous sinus is torn.

Ribs

Whenever a rib fracture is described, the report, in addition to the items mentioned above in the section on general bones, should also state whether the parietal pleura over the fracture is torn. To provide a foundation for later opinions concerning the immediacy of death, the description should mention the degree of bleeding into the endothoracic fascia and intercostal muscles, and give an estimated volume of blood when it is substantial. When ribs are serially fractured, the report should indicate if the muscle and soft tissue of the chest wall are continuously lacerated; this finding implies laceration of the intercostal arteries.

> The left side of the thorax has a serial line of rib fractures laterally, all complete, and a few with pleural laceration. Most are moderately displaced. The adjacent endothoracic fascia and intercostal muscles have an estimated 20 ml of extravasated blood.

For homicides, the report should name each rib that is fractured and give its location in the chest wall as anterior, lateral, posterior, costosternal, or costovertebral.

> Right ribs 1 through 8 at the posterior aspect of the thorax have complete fractures in a serial line. Displacement varies from none to minimal. The pleura over the fractures of the 3rd and 5th ribs is torn. An estimated 5 ml of blood in is the intercostal muscles and endothoracic fascia adjacent to the fractures. Left rib 4 has a complete fracture at the lateral aspect of the thorax, with minimal displacement, no pleural laceration, and almost no blood extravasation.

For accidents, the description can be more of a summary but should still locate the fractures on the chest wall and describe soft tissue injuries.

> The anterior and lateral aspects of the thorax have multiple complete rib fractures bilaterally, with extensive displacement, extensive laceration of the chest wall musculature, and numerous lacerations of parietal pleura; the appearances are those of a stove chest.[1] The adjacent intercostal muscle has less than an estimated 30 ml of extravasated blood.

For rib fractures produced by closed chest compressions during an effort at resuscitation, one can simply state that the thorax has multiple nondisplaced rib fractures anteriorly on both sides and add a parenthetical opinion:

> (Comment: Resuscitation effort).

Long Bones and Pelvis

A fracture of a long bone should be described so as to locate it at the proximal metaphysis, shaft, or distal metaphysis. Pelvic fractures are located to the constituent

---

[1] *Stove chest*, a term more familiar to British than American physicians, is the morphological equivalent of the better-known clinical term *flail chest*. Because a flail chest involves inefficient respiratory excursions, the clinical term is not correct for a trauma victim who dies instantly or lives so briefly that respirations are never observed. *Stove* is the past-tense form of the verb *to stave*.

pelvic bone or area, that is, pubic bone, ischium, ilium, or acetabulum. Sacroiliac joint disruptions are described as lacerations if confined to the joint and if there is no ankylosis. In the elderly, these joint wounds are more often described as fracture dislocations because of partial ankylosis or extension of the joint wound into the sacrum or the os coxae.

In the case of a pedestrian struck by a vehicle that flees the scene, the description of a tibial fracture should indicate which side of the fracture is splintered and which is cleanly broken, in order to provide a foundation for a direction-of-impact opinion. The distance from the fracture to the sole of the foot should be recorded to provide the basis for an opinion as to the height of a bumper at impact.

For open fractures, the report should give the size and location of the overlying cutaneous laceration and indicate whether any deep soft tissue is lacerated.

For fractures of bones not ordinarily exposed by the autopsy procedure, such as the nasal bone and the long bones of the extremities, one should state whether the determination was made by radiograph, palpation, external evidence of dislocation, or direct examination by dissection.

> The nasal bones are palpably fractured, as evidenced by crepitus.

Vertebrae

Wounds of the vertebral column that place the spinal cord at risk usually involve dislocation. Only some involve fractures. It is not adequate to simply state that vertebrae are dislocated. One should describe the wounds of ligaments, disc, dura, and bone that permit the dislocation. The use of the word *fracture* for a laceration of a disc, facet joint capsule, or ligamentum flavum is incorrect. In a case of fracture of a vertebra or laceration of a vertebral ligament, the report should explicitly state whether the joint has any static displacement or distraction of the involved vertebrae. A description of a laceration should be accompanied by a description of the extent and location of any blood extravasation.

The report should indicate whether a vertebral fracture involves the body, lateral elements, pedicles, laminae, or spinous process. For fractures of the vertebral body, one should indicate if the fracture is a compression fracture.

> The neck has a dislocation injury between the 5th and 6th vertebrae. It is manifested by laceration of the anterior longitudinal ligament and the anterior aspect of the underlying intervertebral disc, and sprain of the left C5-6 facet joint capsule. The prevertebral fascia has a thin spot of extravasated blood, as does the anterior longitudinal ligament. The C5 and C6 vertebrae have no static dislocation.

Ligaments, Joints, and Muscle

Although clinicians commonly use the terms *strain* and *sprain,* they are rarely looking at the actual tissue in office practice. *Strain* properly belongs to discussions of

Newtonian mechanics; *sprain* is the preferred nomenclature for blood extravasations in muscle and ligaments when the injury is caused by excessive tensile force rather than direct impact.

Body Cavities

Blood cannot get into a body cavity without going through a hole in the serosa lining the cavity. The pathologist should search for and describe the location of the defect in the serosa. The volume of blood in body cavities should always be measured, to enable subsequent calculations of percentage of total blood volume lost.

Serosal tears of a body cavity should be localized to adjacent anatomical structures. For example, a laceration of parietal pleura can be adjacent to a rib fracture, run in the intercostal space, or involve the mediastinal pleura near an aortic laceration or vertebral dislocation. Lacerations of the pericardial sac are important to describe because they may explain the presence of blood in a pleural cavity from a cardiac wound, and because they may permit the inference that the heart suffered transient herniation through the pericardial defect at the moment of impact, even though there may be no static herniation at the autopsy table.

Great Vessels

Aorta

Most thoracic aortic lacerations also involve the overlying mediastinal serosa and produce immediate bleeding into a body cavity. Others are tamponaded by intact serosa for a while; some of these wounded persons survive to be saved surgically, and some have delayed rupture of the serosa, often at a location that does not directly overlie the aortic laceration. The report should indicate if the mediastinal serosa is torn so as to permit communication between the pleural cavity and the aortic lumen. If the serosa is intact, the laceration was tamponaded and can be labeled as such.

The report should state explicitly whether an aortic laceration permits communication between the aortic lumen and a body cavity, whether the laceration involves the entire circumference or some fraction of the circumference, for example, 3/4 or 90%, and whether the laceration involves the full thickness of the wall or only the intima.

The location of the laceration along the axis of the aorta should be specific. The most common location is just midway between the take-off of the left subclavian artery and the first pair of intercostal arteries. More distal lacerations often accompany underlying vertebral dislocations; if this is the case, the relationship should be explicit.

Other Vessels

In cases of impact trauma, one should describe any sprain wounds of the intrapericardial portion of the inferior vena cava. These are manifested by blood extravasation in the wall without laceration.

Again, with impact trauma, one should describe any lacerations of the inferior vena cava. These tend to occur near the renal vein inflows, are often small compared to the circumference of the cava, and can account for retroperitoneal hematomas.

Dislocation of thoracic vertebrae can cause laceration of the azygous vein where it passes just superior to the right pulmonary hilus. This wound sometimes accounts for a right hemothorax. Such a laceration can be documented after opening the vein with scissors.

Impact to the thorax anteriorly that causes fracturing of the first rib anteromedially can also cause laceration of the internal mammary artery. If one applies the rib cutter to remove the breastplate before thinking of a possible laceration of this artery, it may be torn by the rib cutter. If there is no other source for a sizable right hemothorax, one can opine the laceration as a diagnosis, and state in the description of findings that the proximal part of the internal mammary artery is adjacent to rib fractures and lies in the path of the rib cuts.

Sometime a wound crosses a vessel that is important but cannot be seen with usual dissection techniques. For instance, one may have occasion to describe a full-thickness chest wall laceration that includes serial rib fractures. In such a case, one can add that the laceration involves the regions of the intercostal arteries. Similarly, a gunshot wound of the neck may produce bleeding from branches of the external carotid artery, none of which can be seen with ordinary dissection techniques.

The wound track passes through the region of branches of the left external carotid artery.

Heart

A description of a laceration of the heart should state which chamber is involved, whether the laceration penetrated or perforated the wall of the chamber, and whether the laceration crosses a major epicardial artery.

Thin endocardial hemorrhages in the left ventricle are usually ascribed to catecholamine release, not to impact, and are common sequelae of resuscitation attempts. However, endocardial bleeds in the atria are usually contusions caused by impact.

Central Nervous System

The subdural space is not part of the brain; subdural hemorrhages and brain wounds belong in separate paragraphs. The magnitude of a space-occupying subdural hematoma should be measured by maximum thickness and by volume or weight. Thin hemorrhages of no volumetric significance can be so described.

For subarachnoid hemorrhages, no volume estimate is needed, but one should distinguish thick subarachnoid hematomas of the type caused by ruptured arterial aneurysms from thin subarachnoid hemorrhages caused by head impact, in which the blood merely leaks and stains the fluid. Thin subarachnoid hemorrhages can be described as focal or confluent.

Cerebral contusions should be located not only to the lobe, but also to the superior, lateral, and inferior aspects of the lobe, or to the poles of the lobes. The report should indicate whether a contusion is limited to the cortex or also involves the white matter. Stating the color of the contusion is helpful.

Diffuse axonal injury has no specific direct signs at autopsy. Its diagnosis requires consideration of the initial Glasgow coma score and is usually supported by the finding of small hemorrhages in the white matter (also known as intermediate contusions), lacerations of the corpus callosum, or thin subdural hemorrhages.

Lungs

For contusions of the lungs, one should state whether they are small, medium, or large, and whether accompanied by pleural air blebs. (Note: In most organs, a contusion is represented by extravascular blood. In the lung, a contusion is represented by extravascular blood *and* by extra-alveolar air). A more elegant practice is to estimate the volume of a lung that is involved with contusional blood extravasation. Describing the color of contusions is helpful.

Lacerations of the lung should be located in a lobe. The report should state whether a laceration is pleural-based, hilar, or intraparenchymal. If it is hilar, one should indicate whether arteries and bronchi are involved.

> The lungs have dark red pleural-based contusions involving the upper lobes and occupying an estimated 10% of the total lung volume. The contusions are accompanied by prominent small pleural air blebs. The lingula has a 1 × 1 × 0.5 cm pleural-based laceration corresponding to the above-described rib fracture.

Liver

In the case of multiple liver lacerations, one need not measure and count individual lacerations; a maximum size can be given, along with an estimate of the percentage of the liver volume involved. If the lacerations are extensive, the pathologist should open the hepatic veins before slicing the liver to determine whether any of the hepatic veins are torn. If the lacerations are few, one should state whether the lacerations are mainly capsular or deep.

Spleen

Lacerations of the spleen should be categorized as capsular or deep, and specified as either single or multiple.

Internal Examination

The internal examination is the most informative part of the report for a death by natural causes. It is customarily organized by organ system, in whatever order personally suits the pathologist. If the report is dictated after rather than during the autopsy, it can be composed to optimize communication rather than to reflect the sequence in which the examination was conducted. For instance, although the head is usually opened after the removal of the organs of the thorax, abdomen, pelvis, and neck, one can describe the skull, meninges, and brain first if one dictates after the autopsy.

Autopsy Procedures

Unlike a surgeon's operative report, which focuses on procedures, the autopsy report focuses on findings. The report should not mention ordinary dissection procedures. If asked in deposition, one can discuss the dissection techniques. However, special dissection procedures need to be noted but not described in detail. Most procedures can be implied by a thorough description of the findings. For example:

> A layer-wise posterior neck dissection is negative.

This mentions a procedure and gives no anatomical detail. Better still is the following:

> The broad muscles of the posterior aspect of the neck and the muscles and fasciae of the suboccipital triangles have no blood extravasations. The posterior and lateral elements of the cervical vertebrae and their ligaments and joint capsules have no injuries. The intervertebral discs and the posterior longitudinal ligaments have no lacerations. The spinal canal has no epidural or subdural blood extravasations. The dens, alar ligaments, transverse ligament, and tectorial membrane have no injuries. The spinal cord is intact and has no softenings.

The report should not describe artifact created by dissection unless it is absolutely unavoidable. This may be the case when part of the dissection is done by an assistant and the pathologist does not have enough experience to evaluate the finding. The finding then gets reported and the problem is left for someone else to solve. Delegation of dissection work to non-physicians should be kept to a minimum.

Wounds, Therapy, and Donations

If wounds, therapeutic devices, and organ donations are treated in special sections of the report, they should not be repeated in the internal examination section.

Body Cavities

This is the traditional opening paragraph of the internal examination in which the in-situ observations are recorded. Here one describes the degree of organ congestion and whether the organs are normally *sited*. Many pathologists consistently comment on the presence or absence of abnormal odors. This paragraph is a good place to describe postmortem radiographs if this task has not been accomplished elsewhere. Decompositional changes of organs and fasciae can be summarized here rather than for each organ separately. If they are not described in a separate section, one can use this paragraph to describe the absence of donated organs and the alterations of remaining organs and fasciae.

Gas

The simple technique of scraping intercostal muscle from the outside of the parietal pleura can be used as a test for pneumothorax in every autopsy. One can describe a negative pleural window test or, when there is gas under tension, describe what was seen or felt, such as outwardly bulging intercostal pleura and a downwardly bulging diaphragmatic leaf. By these observations, one can state whether the gas is under tension.

Liquid

The term *bloody effusion* could be construed to mean bloodstained serous liquid, or whole blood. A better practice is to be specific when possible and, for example, state that the cavity has 800 ml of blood. One should indicate if cavity blood is clotted or liquid.

Cavity blood can be described in the body cavities paragraph or in the wound section. If blood in a body cavity results from a single wound, it is more effective to describe the cavity blood immediately after the wound. If the blood in a cavity results from more than one wound, the blood may be more effective to describe it in the body cavity paragraph of the internal examination.

Chest Wall Location

Lesions of the ribs or intercostal spaces are located with respect to sternocostal, anteromedial, anterior, anterolateral, lateral, posterolateral, posterior, posteromedial, costotransverse, or costovertebral aspects of the thorax.

Adhesions

Adhesions of body cavities are classified as fibrinous or fibrous. The latter are old and are usually of interest when intestinal obstruction or respiratory insufficiency results. The former imply an active healing or inflammatory reaction. One should describe the structures connected by adhesions:

> The left lung is connected by fibrous adhesions to the chest wall laterally and to the diaphragm. The left leaf of the diaphragm is tacked up to the chest wall by dense fibrous adhesions.

rather than:

> The left lung has adhesions.

Fibrous adhesions can be taeniaform (tape-like) or confluent. In some cases, one can simply state that a body cavity is obliterated by fibrous adhesions.

Missing Organs

Missing organs should be classified as congenitally absent or surgically absent, and acutely absent or remotely absent. Example:

> The gallbladder is absent due to remote surgery; fibrous adhesions connect the large intestine, duodenum, and stomach to the bed of the previously resected gallbladder and to the liver.

Radiographs

Positive or negative X-ray findings are included when the findings are not adequately conveyed by naked-eye description. Examples of such findings include cardiac gas embolism, negative films in infants, estimated numbers of birdshot, and pelvic fractures.

Heart and Great Vessels

Great Vessels

The cardiovascular paragraphs should mention the aorta, venae cavae, pulmonary trunk, and pulmonary arteries. The azygous and hemiazygous veins and the internal mammary vessels should be examined if blood in the pleural cavities cannot be explained by more obvious sources.

The report should indicate the contents of the great vessels and chambers of the heart as being liquid blood, clots, gas, or a mixture, and should state whether the chambers and vessels are distended, filled, underfilled, or collapsed. For this purpose, the term *empty* is vague and to be avoided; it could mean "filled with gas" like an empty glass, or "collapsed and empty."

Thromboemboli

For thromboemboli, one should describe the range of diameters of the thromboemboli, the aggregate length of thromboemboli, the presence of venous valve markings, the estimated percentage of the cross-sectional area of the largest artery involved, areas of adherence to arterial walls, and the color of the thromboemboli. Most are dark purple, with a grayish surface. The description should also include the names and levels of the arteries involved, such as pulmonary trunk, main pulmonary artery, lobar arteries, segmental arteries, and subsegmental arteries. One should state whether the left or right lung is more heavily involved and whether or not the lungs have infarctions.

Epicardial Arteries

The description of the coronary arteries should include the ostia and either give the distribution pattern (right, left, or nondominant) or describe the branching pattern of the arteries (e.g., the posterior descending artery arises from the right coronary artery). The left main artery must be included in the description either explicitly or implicitly. The patency of the arteries is described; this can be done with a one-sentence description for normal arteries but may require a full paragraph for diseased arteries.

Coronary Bypass Grafts

A coronary graft should be described so as to include the location of its origin at the aorta and the names of the epicardial arteries receiving anastamoses. The description should state whether the graft is patent or obstructed and whether the graft is made of a vein or an artery.

Assessing Luminal Obstruction

The degree of obstruction of a coronary artery is usually given as a percentage of the cross-sectional area. The degree of obstruction is more meaningful if one also states whether the artery has compensatory dilation. The practice on the part of pathologists of estimating percentage obstruction is borrowed from the radiologists. Interestingly, radiologists do not really measure the percentage of luminal obstruction; they compare luminal diameters. However, luminal diameter may be a more useful datum than percentage obstruction. For example, if an arterial segment has a 10-mm diameter and is 75% obstructed, leaving a 3-mm lumen, the flow might be adequate. If a 2-mm artery has a 75% obstruction, the lumen is a pinpoint and flow is poor. Measuring the actual diameter of the lumen is helpful in creating a word picture of the lesion.

Plaques

The description of atherosclerotic plaque in a coronary artery optimally includes color, calcification, hardness, and the concentric or eccentric disposition of the plaque. For a thrombus, the description should include the length of the thrombus, whether it is adherent and distending the artery, whether it is mural or occlusive, and whether it is gray, pink, or red. The color indicates whether the thrombus is platelet-rich or red cell-rich, which in turn indicates whether the thrombus formed in a brisk or sluggish stream of blood.

Myocardium and Chambers

The determination of left ventricular hypertrophy rests on the appearance of the heart sections and on the weight of the heart. Because the weight of the heart is key, a good practice is to include with the measured heart weight the *expected weight*. This is easily accomplished by inserting a parenthetical comment after the pathologic heart weight. Furthermore, if the heart weight is increased, the report should state why. If the reason is left ventricular hypertrophy, one should state whether the hypertrophy is concentric.

> The heart weighs 540 grams (Comment: The expected heart weight for this 198-pound man is less than 400 grams). The increased weight is caused by concentric left ventricular hypertrophy.

The cut surfaces of the myocardium should be described sufficiently to indicate if they have recent or old infarctions. Measuring the ventricular wall thickness is useful in selected fixed hearts. Wall thickness can be omitted in the majority of adult autopsies because it does not add any diagnostic information to the combination of heart weight and degree of chamber dilation.

The chronic dilation of any chamber should be described.

Myocardial Infarction

The description of a myocardial infarction should indicate whether the lesion is an old scar or a recent necrosis; whether it is accompanied by any aneurysmal dilation or cavitary thrombus; whether the infarction is subendocardial or transmural (transmural is defined as anything more than 50% of the wall thickness); whether it is posterobasal, anteroseptoapical, lateral, or more localized; and should include an overall surface dimension in centimeters. Scars less than 1 centimeter wide are unlikely to have been clinically diagnosed as infarctions and are best labeled as foci of myocardial fibrosis rather than as infarctions. The description should always indicate whether an infarction involves a papillary muscle, because the loss of papillary muscle function causes mitral insufficiency and congestive heart failure.

Valves and Endocardium

The description of the heart should always mention the valves and the endocardium. For diseased valves, the description should be written so that the reader can imagine the degree of stenosis or regurgitation. If a valve is thickened, one should state whether the thickening is caused by fibrosis, myxoid change, or another process. If a valve has fusion of its parts, the report should describe the exact structures involved, such as commissures.

Lungs

Bronchial content should be described so as to include any mucus, pus, mucopus, gastric fouling, gastric-fouled mucus, blood, or froth. The description of bronchial content should include color; should indicate whether the material is in mainstem, lobar, segmental, or subsegmental bronchi; and should state whether the material lines or occludes the lumens. *Mucopurulent material* is a soft, ambiguous term and should be avoided in favor of the more straightforward *mucopus*.

Pulmonary Arteries

One should mention the patency of the intrapulmonic arteries.

Cut Surfaces

The report should describe the degree of crepitance or aeration, the color, and the consistency of the cut surfaces. Emphysematous changes should be described well enough to indicate whether the emphysema is centrilobular, paraseptal (bullous), or some other type, and should indicate whether the changes are early or advanced. The earliest indication that purulent bronchitis has evolved to bronchopneumonia may be that the cut surfaces are intensely congested and somewhat lumpy.

> The pleural membranes have no adhesions or exudates. The bronchi are filled by pink froth. The pulmonary arteries have no thromboemboli. The cut surfaces have the tattered loss-of-tissue appearance characteristic of centrilobular emphysema; this change is most prominent in the upper lobes. The cut surfaces have tobacco staining manifested by green spots in a centrilobular distribution. The cut surfaces range from dry and gray anteriorly to dark red and congested posteriorly.

Liver, Bile Ducts, Gallbladder, and Pancreas

Liver

The description of the liver should mention the capsule and the cut surfaces. If the liver is swollen, the inferior margin is rounded or blunt. Conversely, in a liver that is not swollen, the inferior margin is sharp. One should estimate the volume of liver occupied by any tumor nodules.

Bile Ducts

If the common bile duct is dilated, one should explore it for obstructions and, if there are none, say so.

Gallstones

The report should indicate the color, consistency, size, estimated number, and shape of any concretions. In general, pigment stones are crumbly and mixed composition stones are hard.

Pancreas

The parenchyma should be mentioned. Ducts should be mentioned if dilated.

Reticuloendothelial System

The description of the spleen should mention the capsule and the cut surfaces and include the color and consistency. Bone marrow, lymph nodes, the thymus, and the palatine tonsils should be mentioned.

Genitourinary System

Prostate Gland and Seminal Vesicles

For the description of the prostate, one should indicate whether it is enlarged or nodular, and give an estimated diameter or weight if it is enlarged. The seminal vesicles should be mentioned.

Kidneys

The description of the kidneys should mention the cortical and cut surfaces. The cortices are often described as smooth, granular, or scarred. The cut surfaces are described with respect to color and any grit or gravel. If the kidneys are small or granular, one should indicate whether the cortices are reduced in thickness. For cysts, the description should be in enough detail to permit another pathologist to decide if the kidney has multiple simple cysts or polycystic kidney disease. This can be done with a parenthetical opinion.

Urinary Bladder

The description of an undiseased urinary bladder can be limited to the estimated volume and character of its contents.

Testes

The cut surfaces should be mentioned, and the report should indicate whether the testes are descended or missing.

Endocrine Organs

The description of the endocrine organs should mentions the adrenal, thyroid, and pituitary glands and do it in such a fashion that it is clear whether the pituitary was removed from the sella for the examination. The report should mention color. Involution of the fetal adrenal cortex is common in infants and can resemble hemorrhage. An enlarged parathyroid should be mentioned if it is observed. Most autopsies do not require a search for all parathyroid glands.

Digestive Organs

Serosa

Parts of the gut have a serosal lining on the outside and parts do not. The term *serosa* should not be used for the adventitia of a segment that has no serosa. The esophagus has no serosa except in emaciated persons, whereas the stomach always does. The duodenum is partly invested with serosa (see below). The jejunum and ileum are completely invested with serosa except for the mesenteric border. The large intestine is partly invested with serosa, the transverse colon and sigmoid colon being fully invested, the rectum not at all, and the remainder partly and variably.

Esophagus, Stomach, and Duodenum

One should mention the presence or absence of chronic ulcers. If there is an ulcer, one should give a diameter, a depth, and a location in the organ, and state whether it is penetrating or perforating. If the ulcer is penetrating, the report should indicate to what level of tissue it penetrates and whether there is an arterial stump in the base.

Lesions in the esophagus are located to the proximal, mid- or distal esophagus, and lesions in the stomach are related to the anterior wall facing the peritoneal cavity, the posterior wall facing the omental bursa; the greater curvature or the lesser curvature; and to the cardiac, body, and antral regions. Duodenal lesions are related to the antrum, the ampulla, and the post-ampullary duodenum; and to a free wall versus a wall abutting the pancreas.

If there is a lesion of the esophagus, the report should indicate whether the lumen is obstructed and estimate the diameter of the lumen at the lesion. The measured volume and character of the gastric contents are reported.

Intestines

The report should mention the small and large intestines.

Lesions in the small intestine should be localized to the jejunum, mid-small bowel, ileum, or terminal ileum. Lesions in the large intestine are localized to one of its named segments. The term *large intestine* is not synonymous with *colon*. The colon is one part of the large intestine; the other three parts are the cecum, appendix, and rectum. One should localize lesions in the colon to one of its four parts: ascending, transverse, descending, and sigmoid.

In casual speech, surgeons refer to the large bowel mesentery. Strictly speaking, only the small bowel has a mesentery. The large bowel has two mesocolons. The autopsy report should specify the transverse mesocolon or the sigmoid mesocolon.

It is not necessary to mention that the appendix is present or absent unless identification is an issue.

Musculoskeletal System

This section should mention the ribs, clavicles, sternum, vertebral column, and pelvis. Radiographs are described if doing so adds to the pathological description. A general comment about the musculature is sufficient if the musculature is unremarkable; for the purposes of the internal examination, it is understood that observations are limited to the musculature of the neck, thorax, abdomen, and pelvis unless some special dissection is described.

If the popliteal and leg veins are examined, the report should include the extent of the examination (usually the popliteal and interosseous leg veins), the presence or absence of clots, whether any venous clots are retracted or bulging, or adherent to the intima, and whether the leg fascia is edematous.

Neck

The paragraph for the neck should mention the vertebral column, strap muscles, larynx, tongue, and the contents of the upper airways, indicating whether the lumen is lined or occluded by foreign material. If a posterior neck dissection is performed, the report should make it obvious by describing, at least for negative examinations, some of the deepest structures examined.

Obstruction of Airway by Foreign Body

The description of food lodged in the upper airway should include an estimate of the percentage obstruction of the cross-sectional area, and should indicate whether the bolus is firmly or loosely lodged and whether the focus of lodgment is the pharynx or the larynx. The bolus should be briefly described as meat or other recognizable food, including color and texture. If one gives the superior range of the bolus as above the epiglottis, it would be useful to give the lower limit as, for example, below the glottis.

Swelling

An epiglottis swollen by anasarca should be descriptively distinguished from an epiglottis that is the seat of localized edema.

Head

For a head with no lesions, the report should mention the following: galea, vault of skull, base of skull, epidural space, dura mater, subdural space, leptomeninges, cerebral arteries, cranial nerves, and the external and cut surfaces of the brain. If the brain is fixed for subsequent description, it should be mentioned here.

Berry Aneurysms

Ruptured berry aneurysms produce thick subarachnoid hematomas that displace the cerebrospinal fluid and distend the cisterns. One should further describe whether the blood extends down the spinal canal or up the sides of the cerebrum. With respect to the aneurysm itself, it is helpful to report the direction in which the aneurysm projects, such as anteriorly, toward the base of the skull, or posteriorly. Blood adherent to the adventitia of the aneurysm should be described because it points to recent leakage of blood.

Cerebral Atherosclerosis

If the cerebral arteries have atheromas, one should describe their extent and distribution in general terms. Specification of the percentage obstruction of the lumen is unnecessary because there are no benchmarks for such data.

Tumors

The description of tumors should include size, color, texture, necrosis, and circumscription; degree of obstruction of any involved hollow organ; and percent by volume of solid organs. For the size of a round tumor in a solid organ, a single, greatest dimension is usually enough. For tumors of irregular shape, three dimensions are needed to indicate the size.

Chapter 2
Opinion Reports

The Logic of Opinion Formation

To help the reader better understand the structure of the opinion section of the autopsy report that is described subsequently, a brief review of the logic of opinion formation is in order.

Definitions of Cause, Mechanism, and Manner

Diagnosis

The term *diagnosis* can be most simply defined as the thing that is wrong with the patient or the thing that was wrong with the decedent. A diagnosis can be expressed in morphological, pathophysiological, or public health–related terms, and it can reflect basic etiology or tertiary derangements of physiology. Note that postmortem changes are not diagnoses. For example, putrefactive decomposition is a postmortem change, not a diagnosis. (When it occurs in a living person, it takes a different name, that is, gangrene, which *is* a diagnosis.)

Cause of Death: Definition

The *cause of death* is the underlying disease or injury that begins the pathophysiological train of events that culminates in the electrical silence of the heart and brain. A competent cause of death is etiologically specific, that is, it gets to the root of the matter.

Cause of Death: Medical Versus Legal

Physicians certify an *underlying* cause of death. Attorneys often speak of a *proximate* cause of death. The two concepts are related but are not the same. Physicians should avoid referring to the underlying cause of death as the proximate cause of death. For example, an elderly woman slips in a puddle at the grocery store, falls, sustains a fracture of the femoral neck, and dies of the medical sequelae of the

V.I. Adams, *Guidelines for Reports by Autopsy Pathologists,*
© Humana Press, Totowa, NJ 2008

fracture. The underlying cause of death is the fracture of the femoral neck. For the plaintiff attorney, the proximate cause of death is the slip on the wet floor.

Cause of Death: Immediate, Intermediate, and Underlying

Often, the cause of death is broken out into immediate and underlying causes of death. Sometimes intermediate causes of death are employed, especially when the duration of survival is long:

> Urinary sepsis due to
> Laceration of spinal cord with paralysis due to
> Fracture-dislocation of vertebral column at T4-T5 due to
> Blunt impact to torso

Mechanism

The *mechanism of death* is the physiological derangement set in motion by the disease or injury. Examples of mechanisms of death include cerebral edema, pulmonary edema, sepsis, ventricular fibrillation, and hemorrhagic shock. Note that each of these entities can result from a wide variety of underlying diseases and injuries. When clinical physicians ask for the cause of death, they usually want the mechanism of death. More often than not, the mechanism of death is either invisible to the morphology-based pathologist or must be inferred from the morphological clues or the terminal circumstances. In a monitored patient in an intensive care unit, the physiological derangement is often spelled out. For deaths outside the hospital, the scene investigation is important in providing information that helps to include or exclude potential mechanisms of death. A mechanism of death can be employed on occasion as an immediate cause of death if it serves the purpose of communication (see the example above of urinary sepsis).

Manner of Death

The *manner of death* is a quasi-judicial classification scheme that dates back centuries. Five manners of death are employed: *natural, accident, suicide, homicide*, and *undetermined*. A natural death is caused exclusively by disease. If any kind of injury contributes to death, be it mechanical, chemical, or by any kind of physical agency, the manner of death is not natural. An exception is the category of therapeutic complications. For a person who dies of an underlying disease, the mechanism of death is always a complication of the disease, a complication of treatment, or a combination of the two.

Manner-of-death determination is a tool that can assist in cause-of-death determination. Usually, the manner of death follows logically from the cause of death and the circumstances. For example, a man has a sudden death on the golf course in view of witnesses. The autopsy shows heart disease and no trauma, and there is no intoxication.

The cause of death is the heart disease, which, being a disease, makes the manner of death natural.

In some cases, the cause of death follows logically from the manner of death, and the manner of death from the circumstances. For example, the partly skeletonized body of a prostitute is found in a wooded area, without clothing. The autopsy, to the extent that it can, shows no disease or trauma. Based on the circumstances, the pathologist will start with the rebuttable presumption that the death is unnatural, probably a homicide. The cause of death is then some form of homicidal violence that did not leave marks on the skeleton. Strangulation would be a reasonable possibility as the cause of death.

Global Approach

At the turn of the 20th century, clinicians made diagnoses based on symptoms and signs, and autopsy pathologists made diagnoses based on morphological findings. Clinicopathological correlation was simple: The clinician guessed the diagnosis, and the pathologist either confirmed or refuted it. As the 20th century unfolded, clinical physicians began actively managing the physiology of their patients, and the hospital records of patients became more complex. Meanwhile, autopsy pathologists remained attached to the morphology-based paradigm. Not surprisingly, the opinions of autopsy pathologists became less and less useful to clinicians as the decades wore on.

In the late 1940s and the 1950s, two leading forensic pathologists began to realize the limitations of the morphology-based approach to autopsy diagnosis. Dr. Lester Adelson, working in Cleveland, sorted autopsies into four classes, depending on the degree to which morphology, rather than circumstances and ancillary tests, controlled the cause-of-death opinion.[1]

Dr. Joseph Davis and his associates, working in Miami, made a similar change of approach, but also broke free of the idea that autopsy findings were somehow superior to other forms of information deriving from the circumstances, medical history, or ancillary postmortem tests.[2]

Think Like a Physician

The Miami pathologists arrived at a simple conclusion: The autopsy pathologist must think like any other physician. The classic paradigm for making a clinical diagnosis involves the physician taking a history from the patient, performing a physical examination, and then ordering laboratory tests and radiographs. As data are added at each step in this process, the physician modifies a list of possible diagnoses (the differential diagnosis). Some new diagnoses are added, and some are excluded at various steps. If the list is not pared down to one likely diagnosis by the last step,

---

[1] Adelson L. No anatomic cause of death. *Conn. State Med. J.* 1954;18:732.

[2] Wright RK and Wetli CV. A guide to the forensic autopsy—Conceptual aspects. *Pathol. Ann.* 1981;16:273–288.

the physician expands the history taking, performs more lab tests, and orders more radiographs until only one working hypothesis is left.

A good autopsy pathologist follows a similar process. The pathologist first gathers information from the medical and social history, and learns the circumstances of death (what the decedent was doing when he or she died). Based on this historical information, the pathologist gains an idea of whether the death is likely to have been caused acutely by a cardiovascular disease, slowly by a chronic disease, or perhaps by the delayed effects of remote trauma. The autopsy and postmortem laboratory tests are customized accordingly to gather the most pertinent information. If a conclusion has not been reached after the first pass through this algorithm, the pathologist seeks more medical history or circumstantial facts, performs additional histological studies, or performs more ancillary laboratory tests, until only one reasonable hypothesis remains. That becomes the opinion.

This approach has been captured in different words by several pithy axioms:

> *The autopsy is just another laboratory test.*
> *The autopsy does not give the cause of death.*
> *Think like a doctor, not like a surgical pathologist.*

Synthesis of Cause, Mechanism, and Manner

The global approach to cause-of-death determination requires that the pathologist, while working through the various phases of an investigation, be thinking not only of causes of death, but also of possible mechanisms of death, and manners of death. Just as the pathologist refines hypotheses concerning the cause of death as the investigation proceeds, he or she also considers and refines hypotheses concerning the mechanism and manner of death. Consideration of each of the three elements can help to discern the others.

Competing Diseases and Injuries

When a pathologist must sort out multiple competing causes of death, it is helpful to ask a few standard questions.

Circumstances

What was the decedent doing when he or she died? Asking this question can solve many cases. The question focuses the investigation on the circumstances and, therefore, on the likely mechanism of death.

Common Mechanism of Death, or Competing Mechanisms?

If two different causes of death are under consideration, they may have complementary or competing mechanisms. For example, an autopsy reveals chronic heart disease, and the toxicology testing reveals parent cocaine and heroin. Was the death caused by a combination of heart disease, intoxication by cocaine, and intoxication by heroin? Not likely. To sort this out, one must focus on the likely mechanism of death by focusing on the terminal circumstances. If the decedent had a sudden, witnessed collapse to a pulseless state, the mechanism is a ventricular arrhythmia. Heart disease and cocaine intoxication commonly kill by means of ventricular arrhythmias, but heroin kills by respiratory depression. With these circumstances, death was most likely caused by the combined effects of the heart disease and the cocaine intoxication. However, if the terminal event was that of a decedent who took cocaine and heroin, and two hours later fell asleep, became unarousable, and was later found dead in bed, the likely mechanism is one of slow death by respiratory depression, and the cause of death is intoxication by heroin.

The Exclusion Test

Sometimes when confronted by multiple disease or injuries, it is helpful to ask for each one: But for this disease, would death have occurred? For example, a man with arteriosclerotic heart disease and paralysis from a remote spinal cord injury dies with urinary sepsis. The question "Absent the heart disease, would this man have died?" in the absence of other information would be answered yes, and the heart disease would not be considered contributory to the death.

Statistical Prevalence

The prevalence of a disease can play a role in determining the etiology of a finding. For example, left ventricular hypertrophy in the absence of valvular disease or myocardial scarring, when found in a 65-year-old, is reasonably ascribed to essential hypertension, even in the absence of a clinical history of hypertension, because essential hypertension has a high prevalence. The same finding of left ventricular hypertrophy in a 22-year-old would invite consideration of hypertrophic cardiomyopathy, because that condition, although not common at that age, is more common than essential hypertension.

The Trigger Concept

The trigger concept is useful, particularly when dealing with the combined effects of chronic disease and acute injury. For example, most persons who die as a result of a fracture of the femoral neck are aged and have multiple chronic diseases. Although some die from direct effects of the fracture such as hemorrhagic shock or fat embolism, most die from exacerbations of natural disease that are triggered by the fracture. When this is the case, the cause of death is ascribed to the disease and the fracture, as a triggering event, is considered a contributory cause of death.

Degree of Certainty

In a criminal trial, the standard for the degree of certainty for an expert opinion is to a reasonable degree of medical certainty, otherwise phrased as a "reasonable degree of medical probability." This requires that the idea being presented as an opinion be more likely than not, that is, probable, and that there be no other competing reasonable possibilities. The latter requirement is derived from the legal requirement in the United States that a jury have no reasonable doubt when finding a defendant guilty.

In a civil trial, the standard for expression of an expert opinion is also expressed as a reasonable degree of medical certainty or probability. In civil suits, this means more likely than not, or probable. Unlike criminal trials, other reasonable possibilities can coexist.

The degree of certainty required for the expression of opinions on a death certificate or in an autopsy report depends on the likely use to which the opinions will be put. Homicide reports generally require opinions to be to the criminal standard. As a matter of practicality, this is also the case for suicides. Rarely, the pathologist may decide that a death was probably a homicide but that other reasonable possibilities cannot be ruled out. In this situation, the pathologist has two options: (1) Opine an undetermined manner of death, or (2) opine a homicide. The latter option, where the pathologist essentially has reasonable doubt about his or her own opinion, requires the pathologist to immediately convey to the prosecutor and detective what the degree of certainty is. For accidents and natural deaths, the civil standard is usually adequate, although in many of these cases it is not hard to meet the criminal standard.

Reasonable possibilities that do not rise to the level of an opinion sometimes need to be included in a report. In an autopsy report, these are often set off as parenthetical remarks in the body of the protocol, using words to indicate the level of certainty, such as *consistent with*. Reasonable possibilities can be worked into summary and opinion reports (see Chapter 2. Opinion Reports; Diagnoses in a Narrative Format; Opinions; Opinions to Omit or Reserve for a Later Time [*page 55*]) or autopsy reports (see Chapter 4, Style; Construction; Inserting Minor Opinions [*page 68*]).

Diagnoses in a Tabular Format

Autopsy opinions, that is, diagnoses, can be expressed in the form of a *tabular list* or in the form of a *narrative* composed of complete sentences. Opinions constructed in the tabular style may appear as the *front sheet* of the autopsy report, or they may appear at the end of the report. The tabular list is the traditional format for expressing autopsy diagnoses.

When employed, a narrative autopsy opinion is usually written as a supplement to tabular-style diagnoses. It usually includes a summary of the hospital course or the circumstances of death. In this book, narrative opinion reports are called *summary and opinion* reports.

Purpose

The purpose of the one-page tabular listing of diagnoses is simple: to convey the essence of the important diagnoses at a glance.

Structure

Two options exist for summarizing an autopsy report in a tabular list.

The *final diagnosis* format lists diagnoses that include opinions based on the medical history, social history, and circumstances as well as the autopsy protocol, toxicology tests, microscopic examination, and ancillary laboratory tests.

The *autopsy findings* format merely lists the important autopsy findings in a tabular format and makes no attempt at integrating circumstantial and autopsy diagnoses. This type of list is helpful if the autopsy protocol is not well organized. However, if the autopsy protocol is well organized, there is little need for a list of the findings.

In this book, the final diagnosis format is presented and preferred. With this format, the final diagnoses are listed on a separate page from the descriptive autopsy findings, in order to cleanly separate the subjective opinions from the objective morphological findings.

The diagnoses are arranged in tabular style, with important or acute lesions expanded by indented entries. An example:

Blunt Impact to Head
    Basilar skull fracture
    Contusions of brain
Arteriosclerotic Heart Disease
    Coronary atherosclerosis
    Multiple (2) remote myocardial infarctions
    Compensatory left ventricular hypertrophy
    Chronic atrial fibrillation (anamnestic)
    Lethal ventricular arrhythmia (opinion)
Cerebral atherosclerosis
Aortic atherosclerosis
Nephrosclerosis
Benign prostatic hyperplasia

The list of diagnoses reads better if it is organized by a logical scheme. More than one scheme can be used simultaneously. Logical schemes can include any of the following:

> *By importance: diseases and wounds pertinent to cause of death at the top, others below.*
> *By chronology: acute diseases at the top, chronic at the bottom.*
> *Mixed: diagnoses by importance, and subdiagnoses by chronology.*

For blunt impact trauma, it is convenient to use the phrases *blunt impact to head*, *blunt impact to torso*, and *blunt impact to extremities* as diagnoses, and to then list the fractures, lacerations, and contusions as subdiagnoses.

Diagnoses that are lifted in their entirety from the medical record are indicated by the parenthetical tag *anamnestic, clinical*, or *history*.

For a diagnosis of a ventricular arrhythmia that is based on a consideration of the circumstances, not on a cardiogram, the parenthetical tag *opinion* provides some guidance to the clinician who might wonder how a morphologist made a physiological diagnosis.

Examples of the tabular final diagnosis format appear in Appendices 1, 2 and 3.

Diagnosis or Finding?

The pathologist must distinguish diagnoses from findings, to support the separation of the subjective from the objective parts of the report (see page 1).

Postmortem wounds are not diagnoses, because they are not problems experienced by the living decedent. They should not appear on the front sheet. These sorts of findings can be identified as postmortem changes by the use of parenthetical comments within the text of the protocol.

For example, with hangings, the *furrow* is an autopsy finding; the diagnosis is *hanging*, or *external ligature compression of the neck*.

In the brain, *white matter hemorrhages* are findings that support the diagnosis of *diffuse axonal injury*.

One cannot have a diagnosis of a pneumothorax or subcutaneous emphysema without antemortem respirations. However, one can have a finding of a pneumothorax or subcutaneous emphysema caused by postmortem mechanical ventilation of a wounded thorax.

Sometimes the distinction between a finding and a diagnosis is blurred. *Hepatomegaly with passive congestion* could be considered either a finding or a diagnosis. A useful practice is to use the phrase *shock liver* if the liver has necrosis. If there is no hepatic necrosis microscopically, congestive hepatomegaly is usually considered a mere finding not important enough for the front sheet.

Some findings are usefully mixed into the list of diagnoses to further clear communication. The use of brief but important morphological findings as indented entries on the front sheet is especially useful for heart disease, as in the example of left ventricular hypertrophy given above. However, this should not be taken as an invitation to load the front sheet with descriptive clutter. Percent obstruction of coronary arteries and the measured thickness of the left ventricle are findings that belong in the descriptive protocol and not on the front sheet.

What to Include

A common mistake by pathologists who perform few autopsies is to blur the distinction between the list of diagnoses and the description of findings by larding the list of diagnoses with descriptive detail that properly belongs in the protocol. The goal for the front sheet is to produce a tabular list that can be scanned in a few seconds to convey an overview of the case. Achieving this goal requires the elimination of clutter on the page.

Degrees of severity, such as mild, moderate, or severe, are useful in the descriptive protocol but have no place on the front sheet. If a disease is mild, one can ask whether it belongs on the front sheet at all. Similarly, the laterality of a lesion need not be stated on the front sheet unless there is a compelling point to be made.

Not all medically or forensically significant diagnoses belong on the front sheet. A medically significant diagnosis can be considered a lesion that would require treatment in a living person. Minor diagnoses not related to the cause of death and that would have been of no clinical import can be left in the descriptive protocol. For example, coronary atherosclerosis should be listed on the front sheet only if the plaques would have been potentially lethal. *Meckel's diverticulum* and *accessory spleen* are not significant diagnoses.

Deaths caused by motor vehicle crashes often produce such a multiplicity of wounds that the list of diagnoses needs to be pruned to achieve clarity. Listing all of the cutaneous contusions in a victim of a traffic crash usually constitutes diagnostic clutter. Subdural hematomas and subarachnoid hemorrhages of no measurable volume can be omitted if the brain is lacerated.

Cause of Death as Diagnosis

Any diagnosis that appears in the cause-of-death opinion should appear in the list of diagnoses. This would appear to be stating the obvious, but in practice this aspect of proofreading is often overlooked.

When the examination is limited to an inspection of the external surfaces, that is, when the body is not autopsied, the pathologist often must use broad, general terminology for the cause of death. The terms *arteriosclerotic cardiovascular disease* and *arteriosclerotic and hypertensive cardiovascular disease* encompass cerebral, cardiac, and peripheral vascular disease and are useful when the underlying but not the immediate cause of death is known. One can use these terms when the circumstances are consistent with either a stroke or a heart attack. For a case involving an autopsy, more specific diagnostic terms such as *arteriosclerotic and hypertensive heart disease* are preferable.

Completeness and Etiologic Specificity

Constructing a complete list of diagnoses requires a conscious effort to find all the pertinent diagnoses by combing through the clinical history, the circumstances, the gross and microscopic autopsy findings, the toxicology report, ancillary lab reports, and the cause-of-death opinion.

To make a list of trauma diagnoses readable for non-physicians, the pathologist should include the name of the organ in a diagnosis. Examples include diffuse axonal injury *of brain,* and laceration of *brainstem* rather than laceration of pontomedullary junction.

The cause of death should always be stated in terms of the underlying disease. In other words, the cause-of-death opinion should be etiologically specific. When an immediate cause of death is known but the underlying cause cannot be determined, one should so state, for example, with the phrase *etiology undetermined.* Etiology can be difficult to determine when the chain of events leading to death is traced back to cirrhosis of the liver, a remote hysterectomy, or obstructive peritoneal adhesions caused by remote surgery, because the next-of-kin may have poor recall after a long interval, or have limited information, or be dead.

Some common diagnostic terms are etiologically nonspecific but are used by clinicians as if they were etiologically specific. For example, *chronic obstructive pulmonary disease* and *chronic obstructive lung disease* are terms based on spirometric tests of lung function and are not etiologically specific. They are useful for external examination cases when the pathologist must rely on the clinical diagnosis. For autopsies, the pathologist must determine by inquiry or examination whether chronic obstructive lung disease is caused by tobacco abuse with resultant chronic bronchitis and emphysema, asthma, or another entity.

Mechanisms of death should be used sparingly as front-sheet diagnoses. A mechanism of death is usefully included as a diagnosis if it helps to communicate an opinion. For example, in the case of a person who dies of liver lacerations on the operating table, *hemorrhagic shock* can be listed as a diagnosis.

Diagnoses in a Narrative Format: The Summary and Opinion Report

The summary and opinion report provides a summary by the pathologist of the hospital course, circumstances of death, autopsy findings, and postmortem laboratory tests and then sets forth the opinions, all in prose form. In many cases, the only opinion given is the cause-of-death opinion, but other opinions can be included in anticipation of future questions. In hospital practice, this type of report is known as the *clinicopathological correlation* or the *epicrisis.* Not all medical examiner offices write prose opinions that incorporate the medical history or circumstances.

Purpose

Records Management

Writing a summary and opinion report enables the pathologist's office to discard voluminous photocopies of hospital records. This saves a considerable amount of shelf space, because the hospital records usually exceed the autopsy records in size.

Case Review

Having a summary and opinion report in the file permits a pathologist other than the case pathologist to rapidly prepare for a conference with surgical colleagues. Similarly, this type of report permits the case pathologist to rapidly reconstruct the rationale behind his or her opinions when a deposition is taken years later. Personally summarizing the hospital course rather than relying on an investigator to do so tends to make the pathologist focus on mechanisms of death, which leads to better-reasoned cause-of-death opinions.

Use by Attorneys

Attorneys welcome even the simplest summary and opinion reports because they are more comfortable with prose opinions than with tabular diagnoses. Some district attorneys request these reports for all homicides.

Handling Complex Sequences

But the most compelling reason for creating such a report is that in many cases the traditional autopsy format of listing diagnoses in a tabular format is not up to the task of communicating the opinions. This is most often the case for deaths involving hospital treatment. Because it lacks verbs, the tabular format is often inadequate for complex treatment sequences over time. The traditional autopsy format was created at a time when the hospital course consisted of a physical examination followed by an autopsy, with no real treatment in between other than bed rest.

Asphyxial Deaths

In most cases of scene deaths, the summary and opinion report adds little to what is conveyed by the front sheet of the autopsy report. However, the reporting of scene deaths that involve suffocation often benefits from the superior ability of complete sentences relative to tabular diagnoses to convey sequences of action and nonmorphological concepts.

Structure

In a typical summary and opinion report, the first paragraph summarizes the essential elements of the circumstances and medical history. The second paragraph summarizes the autopsy findings and postmortem laboratory tests. The third paragraph provides the opinions.

For cases in which the hospital physicians have made all the essential diagnoses, and the autopsy is merely confirmatory, the pathologist can combine the second and third paragraphs (see below).

The preferred verb tense for this type of report is the past tense, except when quoting written records, as in "The record states that . . .." This report should convey the sense of having been the product of thoughtful analysis conducted outside the autopsy room at a later time.

History

Information to Include

The summary of the medical history and treatment should clearly lay out the circumstances of the injury, signs and symptoms, therapy, and original diagnosis in sufficient detail to (1) support the opinions that follow, (2) correlate with the autopsy findings that follow, and (3) preclude the necessity of a colleague pathologist from having to read the hospital records in order to discuss the case with a clinician.

One should always include the initial cardiac rhythm if paramedics were at the scene. Episodes of loss and restoration of vital signs should be included. The summary should indicate whether major changes in vital signs occurred at the scene, en route to the hospital, or in the emergency room.

If the decedent was comatose, the summary should include the initial Glasgow coma score. Finally, the summary must end by explicitly stating that the decedent died. The death event should not be left to implication.

If the autopsy was omitted for a nonnatural death because of an objection to autopsy, one should so state.

Information to Omit

The summary should include only the facts that are used as foundation for the opinions. While the age and sex of the decedent are usually pertinent, race and religion are no longer proxies for socioeconomic status and should be given only if the race or the religion of the decedent is pertinent to the opinions. This is rarely the case. Information that is important for identification of the deceased, for preparation of the demographic portion of the death certificate, or for the purpose of releasing the body and personal effects to the correct next-of-kin belongs elsewhere in a note to the file or in the investigator's report.

A long, complicated course may be summarized if done informatively:

> The subsequent course was one of persistent hypotension, pressor-dependence, and fever, ending with bradycardia and pulselessness.

A layman's summary is not medically informative and should be avoided:

> The patient subsequently declined and was pronounced dead.

Time Intervals and Vital Signs

Including the date of injury but not the date of death conveys no useful information; one should decide whether to include both data points or neither. Similarly, including the time of death in the summary without the time of injury is unhelpful. Routinely providing the name of the hospital and the date and time of death is an exercise in redundancy because these data are usually to be found in the investigator's report or the demographic section of the autopsy report, depending on the reporting format of a particular office.

However, if a time interval is germane to the opinion, the writer can give the interval, or state the beginning and end points. These points can be calendar dates or clock times depending on the survival interval.

Clinical Diagnoses

The major diagnostic impressions of physicians should be included. When they turn out to be correct, one can largely omit their supporting laboratory and radiological findings from the summary, and the autopsy findings from the findings paragraph of the summary and opinion report. This is in contrast to the style of the formal clinicopathological correlation exercises to be found in journals of medicine, in which the laboratory tests are given in detail and the diagnostic impressions of the treating physicians are omitted.

When the clinicians are wrong on a major diagnosis, this should be respectfully highlighted. Otherwise, the correct opinion of the pathologist might remain buried in the autopsy report. On the other hand, quoting paramedic speculations about what the internal wounds might be is rarely useful. It is not uncommon for a paramedic in the field to opine a cervical spinal dislocation when no such injury has occurred.

Order of Presentation

The preferred order for presenting the medical history in a summary of this type is strictly chronological, with the oldest medical and social history first. This practice differs from that of a history and physical examination report on a living person, where it makes sense to go out of order by placing the chief complaint and recent history before the past history.

Autopsy Findings

Information to Include

In the interests of clarity, one should include only the autopsy findings that support the cause-of-death opinion or answer questions likely to be raised by clinicians or others.

Information to Omit

In most cases, one can omit wounds caused by resuscitation efforts when the wounds are essentially postmortem, that is, produced after the cardiac arrest and before the pronouncement of death. The exception would be the case of a decedent who is actually resuscitated. For example, consider the case of a person who collapses pulseless. Resuscitation efforts are entirely without effect and the person is pronounced dead. The pathologist will describe the compression-induced rib fractures in the protocol but will omit them from the summary report, where they could be mistaken for antemortem wounds. For a drug intoxication death, it is sufficient to omit mention of all autopsy findings and simply state that the autopsy revealed no significant wounds or organic disease. It is rarely useful to mention the noncontributory results of bacterial cultures in the summary and opinion report.

If the autopsy findings merely confirm what the clinicians have already diagnosed, one can take the opportunity to be brief, and say just that. For simple reports, the writer can combine the last two paragraphs and simply state, for example, that the autopsy revealed the cause of the cardiac arrest to be arteriosclerotic heart disease.

Opinions

Opinions to Include

The opinion section should always include the cause of death. In many cases, this is the only opinion that is included.

> In my opinion, John Doe died as a result of brainstem laceration due to atlanto-occipital dislocation due to blunt impact to the head.

However, when the hospital course is complicated or has other points of correlative interest, one should try to make this paragraph relate more fully to the foundation laid in the foregoing paragraphs:

> In my opinion, John Doe's cardiac arrest at the scene was caused by neurogenic shock caused by the brainstem laceration. His subsequent course was one of hypoxic encephalopathy following resuscitation from the arrest. The underlying cause of death is laceration of the brainstem caused by atlanto-occipital dislocation due to blunt impact to the head.

In order to recognize the humanity of the decedent, the decedent's name should be used at least once in the text of the opinion.

Including the manner of death is not necessary, but many pathologists include it customarily to add a note of closure. In cases involving a criminal prosecution where the manner of death on the death certificate is other than homicide, one can include a reference to the vital statistics purpose of the manner-of-death certification. For example, in a traffic crash in which a driver flees the scene and is the subject of a criminal investigation, one can write:

> The manner of death, for the purposes of vital statistics registration, is accident.

Opinions to Omit or Reserve for a Later Time

In criminal cases, the initial circumstantial information is often meager, because the witness with the most information, the killer, is not often forthcoming with the details. For this reason, opinions other than the cause of death, if heavily based on the circumstances, are often best reserved to the time of deposition or trial, and not committed to paper at the time of the autopsy.

Pathologists should not make standard-of-care opinions. However, it is acceptable to mention objective findings that will be pertinent to clinical specialists and to introduce reasonable possibilities by stating that one has no opinion on the matter:

> I have no opinion as to whether the apparent drop in hemoglobin was caused by internal hemorrhage or was the result of dilution from venipuncture in a limb with an intravenous infusion.

One should avoid dictating speculative opinions for transcription with the idea of creating a rough draft to work on later. Such drafts are legally discoverable. In other words, if an attorney starts work on a case very early on, he or she might demand the drafts as public records while they exist. If statutes permit, the pathologist should develop a retention schedule that calls for drafts to be discarded when the final reports are signed (see Chapter 6).

Examples of summary and opinion reports are reproduced as Appendices 4 and 5. The summary and opinion format can be compared to the tabular diagnosis format by examining Appendices 3 and 4, which are the final diagnoses and the summary and opinion report on the same death investigation.

Chapter 3
Other Reports

Ancillary Laboratory Reports

Integration and Signature

Integrated Versus Separate Reports

The approach preferred by this guide is to sign an autopsy report that includes the microscopic description and to which the toxicology report is appended. Summary and opinion reports are separate and are issued only to those who request the entire file.

Some forensic pathologists prefer to sign a stripped-down autopsy report that consists only of the gross protocol and the cause-of-death opinion. These pathologists treat the microscopic report and opinions other than the cause-of-death opinion as notes to the file. The advantage to this system is that the district attorney and police receive reports on most homicides faster than they would otherwise; most homicides can be certified as to cause of death without waiting for the microscopic examination or the toxicology report. The disadvantage is that for cases in which numerous correlative diagnoses must be made that depend on microscopic, toxicological, and other laboratory tests, the report that is signed and issued is fundamentally incomplete.

With respect to ancillary laboratory tests such as cultures, serology tests, and biochemical tests, there are two options. Forensic pathologists, for whom the autopsy report is usually only one component of a case file that includes many items such as evidence vouchers, notes from telephone calls, and the like, tend to file ancillary reports in the case folders, and mention them in the autopsy reports only when the results are pertinent. Hospital pathologists, for whom the autopsy report is the sole work product, tend to include all ancillary tests in the autopsy report itself.

The major reason for not publishing ancillary laboratory tests as part of the autopsy report is that for many of these tests, the reference ranges for postmortem results are not the same as the reference ranges for clinical results. A clinical physician who reads a vitreous chemistry test might conclude that the decedent had hyperkalemia, and not realize that the apparently high potassium concentration is simply the result of postmortem leakage from retinal cells. The ideal place to report such tests is in the summary and opinion report, where the text can be expanded as necessary to put the results in the correct perspective.

Signatures: When Required

Autopsy reports must be signed. If reports of histological examination are made separately from the autopsy report, they should be signed by the pathologist. Scene investigation reports should be signed if the narrative is prepared by the pathologist. If the pathologist goes to the scene but does not prepare a report, there is nothing to sign. If the pathologist merely accompanies his own investigator to the scene, the investigator can write and sign the report.

Fixed Organs

The autopsy report should indicate within the protocol if a brain, heart, or other organ was saved in formalin for later examination. This lets the reader know that a neuropathology report may need to be requested. The mention of organ fixation should be accomplished with neutral wording:

> For additional detail, see Description of Fixed Brain Specimen, below.

If the fixed organ report is made by a consulting neuropathologist or cardiac pathologist, it is a separate report that must be signed by the consulting pathologist. If the report is made by the case pathologist, it can be issued as a separate report or, more efficiently, integrated into the autopsy report itself. The practice in the author's office is for the consulting pathologist to provide expertise at the fixed brain dissection conference, and for the case pathologist to write the report, which is then integrated into the autopsy report.

Microscopic Descriptions

In hospital autopsy reports, the microscopic description is almost always integrated into the autopsy report. Many, but not all, forensic pathologists follow this practice.

Although some institutions prefer to integrate the microscopic findings into the gross description, organ by organ, this requires more work by the transcriptionist. For example, noting the date when the slides were read would have to be done again for each organ system. Most pathologists keep all the microscopic descriptions together.

Microscopic descriptions need not be as comprehensive as gross descriptions for a simple reason: The slides themselves serve as the archive of microscopic findings, whereas for the gross findings, the written description is the archive, supplemented in some cases by photographs and diagrams.[1]

Like gross descriptions, microscopic descriptions should, in general, be written so as to answer questions, not raise them.

If the organ or tissue named is non-uniform, one should indicate the region of the organ. For example, the heart has a complex anatomy; a section reported as "Heart: Unremarkable" could have come from a coronary artery, a valve, or myocardium. Better:

Heart: A section of the ventricular septum is unremarkable.

As with gross descriptions, microscopic descriptions may consist only of the diagnostic label for unimportant diagnoses, but should include some description in support of the important diagnoses. Examples:

Prostate gland: Benign hyperplasia.
Lung: Early bronchopneumonia, manifested by mucopus in small bronchi, and sheets of polymorphonuclear leukocytes in some but not all alveoli in the section, with no attendant necrosis.

Scene Investigation by Pathologist

Purpose

The purpose of a visit to the scene of death by a pathologist is threefold: to help the police detectives focus their investigation; to help the pathologist focus the subsequent autopsy investigation; and to be used as the basis for later opinions concerning identification of the lethal weapon, time of death, and postinjury activity of the decedent.

Structure

A scene report consists of three elements: what one is *told* at the scene, what one *observes*, and what one *does*. The observations are conveniently divided into observations of the *environment* and observations of the *body*. The usual report is about one to two pages long and can be dictated in either the present tense or the past tense as long as one tense is used consistently. Present tense is often preferable to avoid constructions like the following:

The house was a single-story house.

Obviously, unless destroyed by fire, the house probably still exists.

---

[1] Consider, however, the situation of the pathologist asked by an attorney to perform a record review, read microscopic slides, and promptly return the slides. The pathologist, knowing that he or she will not be able to see the slides again without considerable effort, will write a much more extensive description than would otherwise be the case.

Case Identification

The header for the scene report does not need to include information such as Social
Security number or date of birth, or any other piece of information that will be in
the investigator's report. The report should include the location of the scene, the date
and time that the pathologist arrived at the scene, the name of the police agency, and
the name of the lead police investigator.

Background Information

This section is for the story of the circumstances as they are told to the pathologist
by the detective at the scene. Because the details of a story often expand and change
as an investigation progresses, it is often useful to reduce the story to its essentials
in order to avoid the later necessity of explaining discrepancies. The report should
include manmade and natural alterations made to the scene before the arrival of the
pathologist, such as opening windows, adjusting the thermostat, moving the body,
removing a wallet, draping the body, or rain. The report should include the time of
the incident, or the time the body was found. A convenient proxy for the latter is the
time of any call to emergency services.

Environment

If time of death will be an important consideration, then some sense of the recent
temperature is useful to convey, even if it is a word description such as "cool and
dry." For an indoor scene, the report can indicate whether the premises are air-
conditioned or heated. If the scene is in a building, one ought to state what kind
of building, and which room. One need not repeat all the detail that will appear
in police reports concerning the contents of rooms. The pathologist will generally concentrate on the physical environment near the body. Much of the detail
concerning the objects in the room will appear in the police report and the scene
photographs.

The police customarily refer to compass points in their reports. This can be useful
outdoors, but for the pathologist is rarely helpful indoors. If compass points are
used as referents for a location inside a building or vehicle, one must then orient the
contents of the building or vehicle to compass points. For example, it does no good
to state that the head is at the north end of the bathtub if one does not state that the
drain is at the south end of the tub. It is simpler to use recognizable items as indoor
referents.

Blood spatter should be described as to location and can be briefly described as
fine, medium, or coarse. Detailed descriptions are not necessary unless the pathologist has special expertise in the interpretation of blood spatter.

Body

This section is essentially an external examination of the body. However, it has a different focus than the external examination conducted as part of the autopsy. In contrast to the autopsy report, the scene report will have more detail on rigor, livor, temperature, decomposition, insects, clothing, and personal effects, not only because the scene is the best place and time to make these evaluations, but because the signs of death cannot readily be ascertained from photographs. Less detail is recorded for the wounds and identifying features, because they will be covered in the autopsy. In the case of multiple bodies, one can designate the bodies as victim #1, #2, and so forth, unless one has the ability to assign permanent case numbers at the scene. The pathologist can later instruct the transcriptionist to insert case numbers and names corresponding to the victim numbers in the scene report.

Actions Taken

This section is optional and is used if the pathologist recovers personal effects, trace evidence, bullets, or other physical evidence at the scene and places them in police custody. Because photographs are always taken at a scene, it is not necessary to use this paragraph merely to state that photographs were taken and the wagon dispatched.

The format described above is designed for the situation in which the interviews of witnesses and the primary processing of the scene are undertaken by lay investigators, either from law enforcement or from the medical examiner office. In those jurisdictions where a physician has primary responsibility for scene investigations, the report format would maintain a more formal separation of information gained from different witnesses.

Appendix 6 is a scene investigation report. It goes with the autopsy report reproduced as Appendix 1.

Animal Bones

Purpose

Law enforcement officers occasionally request consultative assistance to determine whether found bones are human or not. The purpose of the report is simply to document that an examination was made and to provide an opinion that can be used to close out the police case.

Structure

The report should be simple and short. It can combine the findings and the opinion.

Content

The report should first give a count of the number of bones. It should broadly
categorize the bones as long bones, pelvic bones, vertebrae, ribs, or elements of
the skull; whether they are small or large, light and birdlike, or robust; and whether
they have epiphyses. It should state whether the bones are weathered, are putrefied,
or have soft tissue; and whether they have gnaw marks, invasion by rootlets, or
apparent saw cuts or other trauma. Finally, the report should state that the bones
appear non-human. It is not necessary to reach a conclusion as to which species of
animal or bird is represented.

Chapter 4
Style

Construction

Sentences

The objective part of an autopsy report, that is, the protocol, can be conceptualized as a two-column table, with one column for anatomical locations and the other for descriptions of normal or abnormal findings. Each imaginary column is filled with nouns and adjectives. Such a report would have no verbs. Although this sort of format, or various sorts of check-off tables or fill-in-the-blank forms, might be appealing to pathologists, they find little favor with laymen or attorneys for one simple reason: The expression of a thought, idea, or opinion requires a sentence with a subject, a verb, and an object.

Paragraphs

Due to the large number of adjectives and nouns in comparison to the number of verbs, a well-written autopsy report has a high density of information. In other words, it has a high signal-to-noise ratio. Most of the data are static; the report has little or no action. In such a report, short paragraphs are more easily managed and digested by the reader than long paragraphs. One-sentence paragraphs are quite acceptable.

Abbreviations

Before the invention of the printing press, when books were copied on parchment in longhand, abbreviations were a time-, ink-, and parchment-saving convenience to scribes. This is no longer the case. It takes no more effort to utter a phrase into a dictating device than it does to utter the abbreviation for the phrase. Moreover, abbreviations tend to slow the smooth progress of the reader's eye. Furthermore, the meaning and use of abbreviations vary by country, region, and even hospital. For

V.I. Adams, *Guidelines for Reports by Autopsy Pathologists*,
© Humana Press, Totowa, NJ 2008

example, *MI* means myocardial infarction to most American doctors. In Britain, it means mitral insufficiency. For these reasons, abbreviations are unacceptable except for units of measure, such as *cm* for centimeter, or *ml* for milliliter.

Parentheses

Parenthetical expressions are to be avoided unless the material within the parentheses forms a complete thought. Parentheses are useful for the purpose of inserting minor opinions within the descriptive section of the autopsy protocol, as described elsewhere in this guide. The use of parenthetical expressions as adjectives is generally too complex a task to attempt in the course of dictating onto tape. The following actual example highlights one problem with parenthetical expressions, namely, that the antecedent noun is ambiguous.

> The anterior aspect of the ligature furrow is triangular in shape with the apex over the laryngeal prominence (2.7 cm in width), extends superiorly to the base of the jaw (4.0 cm in length).

The object that is 2.7 cm in width could be the furrow or the laryngeal prominence. The object that is 4.0 cm in width could be the furrow or the base of the jaw. Also, this sentence is so complex that the person dictating it lost track of the construction by the time the word *extends* was uttered, and omitted the word *and*.

Adjectives

Strings of Adjectives

In scientific writing, nouns often also serve as adjectives. This can lead to awkward constructions when one attempts serial adjectives. For example:

> ...with a ventricular fibrillation cardiac rhythm.

A preposition or two will smooth out such constructions:

> ...with a cardiac rhythm of ventricular fibrillation.

A string of adjectives is clear only when the adjectives cannot be construed to be anything other than adjectives:

> A small, moist, red-brown abrasion.

Even so, a string of perfectly clear adjectives can still hinder the eye of the reader:

> The anterior lateral right aspect of the chest has a small abrasion.

This construction is improved by moving some of the adjectives aft of the noun and making them adverbs:

> The right side of the chest anterolaterally has a small abrasion.

The latter construction has the advantage of moving the subject closer to the beginning of the sentence, which promotes natural indexing (see below).

Shorthand Adjectives

Shorthand terms created by omitting connecting words might be useful for hand-written notes, but they only detract from formal reports. For example, there is only one back. Rather than dictating "the left back," one can write, "the left *side of the* back."

Free-Loader Adjectives

In an effort to save time, some pathologists express two unrelated ideas in the same sentence by attaching adjectives to an otherwise decent host sentence. The result is a construction that would never occur in speech and reads unnaturally. Examples:

> The heavy purple right lung has a 2-cm firm nodule in the lower lobe.
> The 1250-gram brain has translucent meninges and clear cerebrospinal fluid.
> The edematous conjunctivae have no petechiae.

Better practice is to express two ideas in two sentences:

> The right lung is heavy and purple. It has a 2-cm firm nodule in the lower lobe.
> The brain weights 1250 grams. It has translucent meninges and clear cerebrospinal fluid.
> The conjunctivae are edematous and have no petechiae.

Verbs

Useless and Showy Verbs

With few exceptions, the only verbs needed for the protocol are *is, has*, and *weighs*. All the useful information lies in the nouns and adjectives. The verbs serve only one purpose: to make complete sentences. To achieve a high signal-to-noise ratio, the verbs should be small and inconspicuous. All of the following verb forms are unnecessary:

demonstrates
is evident
evinces
exhibits
examination reveals
are noted
opening of the organ reveals
in place
is present
reveals
is seen

shows
there is *or* there are *to start a sentence*
are without. *Better:* have no

Vague Verbs

In autopsy reports, certain verb constructions can be misunderstood, even in context:

The duct is opened.

In this example, the reader cannot really tell if the duct was opened by the autopsy pathologist in the course of dissection or was previously opened by a surgeon.

The duct has been recently opened.

or

The lumen of the duct is examined by opening it.

are unambiguous. Or, another example:

The hair is cut short.

The use of *cut* here is idiomatic, but imprecise. One could read this and construe it to mean that the pathologist cut the hair, perhaps for the purpose of photographing a lesion. Better:

The hair is about 2 mm long.

or

The pubic hair has been recently shaved.

Similarly:

The front teeth are broken.

The possibilities here include remote fractures, recent damage from intubation, or recent impact trauma. A few extra words would have made the meaning clear.
Another example:

There is no facial hair.

For a male, this could mean that he has pre-adolescent facial hair, is naturally smooth-faced, or that the face is clean-shaven.

Natural Indexing

An easy way to construct descriptive sentences is to start with the anatomical region as the subject of the sentence, connect with *is, are, has,* or *have,* and then describe the lesion or give the pertinent negative. Putting the anatomical region at the beginning of the sentence makes the sentence easy to pick out as one scans the report.

Similarly, when describing an organ, a useful practice is to put the name of the organ in the first sentence to help the layman reader. Example:

> The right lung has a 2-cm firm nodule in the lower lobe.

is easier to pick out of a dense paragraph than

> A 2-cm firm nodule is in the lower lobe of the right lung.

Dictating to Avoid Editing

Proofreading never finds all errors. To avoid the later necessity of combing through the text of the protocol to look for temporary descriptions that must be changed, the efficient pathologist should strive to describe gross lesions in such a way that the descriptions need only minor improvements, rather than wholesale deletions or changes. If, after describing an indeterminate lesion, one adds "This may represent a polyp," the addition raises a question that then seemingly must be answered. Better to omit this sentence. That way, whether or not the microscopic examination puts a diagnostic label on the lesion, one does not have to change the gross description.

Needs to be edited later:

> The liver has a 5-cm nodule (? focal nodular hyperplasia) in the right lobe.

Does not need to be edited later:

> The liver has a 5-cm nodule in the right lobe.

Attorneys' Rules of Construction

When interpreting statutes, lawyers are taught that any list of items is presumed to be complete rather than representative. This is contrary to the customary practice of physicians, where naming several representative structures is taken as evidence of attention to detail. The pathologist can satisfy the lawyers and the physicians with some thought.

For instance, if the description mentions some coronary arteries by name but not others, a lawyer will conclude that the others were not examined:

> The left anterior descending and right coronary arteries have minimal obstruction by soft atherosclerotic plaques. (Left main and left circumflex arteries not mentioned.)

One can separately mention all major epicardial arteries. Or, one can state that the epicardial arteries are all patent with the exception of obstructive plaques in (for example) the anterior descending artery and the right coronary artery, and then go on to describe the plaques.

Another example: In describing the brain, the report mentions the cortex, white matter, basal ganglia, brainstem, and cerebellum. An attorney, prompted by a hired pathologist, might conclude that the autopsy pathologist neglected the thalamus. To avoid this, one can simply state that the external and cut surfaces of the brain are unremarkable.

Inserting Minor Opinions

Some diagnoses are minor and do not belong on the front sheet. Many of these minor opinions concern the effects of therapy. Some diagnoses represent mere reasonable possibilities that do not rise to the level of an opinion. The front sheet can be de-cluttered by inserting these minor opinions as parenthetical comments immediately after the description of the lesion within the body of the protocol:

> The scalp has a large galeal blood extravasation (Comment: antemortem impact vs. artifact of postmortem transport).
> The lateral aspects of the vocal cords have ulcers that penetrate through the mucosa to the underlying cartilage (Comment: intubation).

One can put two reasonable possibilities in a parenthetical comment:

> (Comment: aspiration vs. patchy congestion)

Obviously, if there are two ideas in the comment, they can't both be opinions to a reasonable degree of certainty. This technique is especially useful for lesions that are unimportant and that one cannot diagnose to a reasonable certainty, as in this example:

> A red papule (Comment: insect bite versus dermatosis)

Word Order

Sometimes a reader will infer an unintended causal link from the word order. For example, in a case involving a skull fracture and a craniotomy, if a description of an epidural hematoma follows the description of the craniotomy, most readers will initially think, before reading on, that the epidural blood is caused by the craniotomy. Better to place the epidural blood after the description of the skull fracture if that is what caused it.

The choice of word order can have an effect on the lengthiness of the sentence:

> A 2.5×2.0 cm contusion

is less wordy than

> A contusion measuring 2.5×2.0 cm

This brevity is achieved by placing the measurement before the lesion instead of after. In a report with many measurements, the aggregate effect of this technique can improve the information density.

Terminology

Anatomical Terminology

Mixed Systems of Nomenclature

Systems of surface nomenclature should not be mixed. For example, there is no such thing as a hypogastric or epigastric quadrant. *Hypogastric* and *epigastric* are terms from the nine-square scheme of abdominal surface anatomy. The four quadrants are left upper, left lower, right upper, and right lower.

Terms of Position and Direction

For standard *terms of position or direction*, that is, *anterior, posterior,* and the like, the referent structure must be clear. In the following sentence, it is not clear whether *posterior* refers to the posterior aspects of incompletely fractured ribs or to the posterior aspect of the thorax:

> The 1st, 2nd, and 3rd ribs on the left side of the thorax have nondisplaced posterior fractures.

Better:

> The left side of the thorax posteriorly has a serial line of fractures involving ribs 1, 2, and 3.

Naming the Organ

Naming the organ early in a descriptive paragraph helps to orient the lay reader. A physician can deduce that the involved organ is the brain when the report describes "contusions of the left temporal pole," but the layman cannot.

> The scalp, skull, and meninges have no injuries except as indicated. The epidural and subdural spaces have no blood. The left temporal pole has cortical contusions and thin subarachnoid hemorrhages. The cerebral hemispheres, cerebellum, and brainstem are otherwise unremarkable.

Same information with a better lead-in for the brain description:

> The scalp, skull, and meninges have no injuries except as indicated. The epidural and subdural spaces have no blood. The brain has cortical contusions and thin subarachnoid hemorrhages of the left temporal pole. The cerebral hemispheres, cerebellum, and brainstem are otherwise unremarkable.

Surface Anatomy

Some pathologists use the names of bony and muscular structures as references for surface anatomy without making it clear they are describing cutaneous findings. For example, *deltoid* means the muscle. If the report is describing surface anatomy, *deltoid region* is better.

Latin and Greek

Specificity

In many cases, a Latin- or Greek-based medical term has a specificity that is lacking in the common English word. When this is the case, use the medical term. However, when the English term is just as specific as the Latin, use the English term to make the report more readable to nonmedical persons. Thus, use *nostril(s)* rather than *naris* and *nares*. Similarly, *finger* rather than *digit*.

Singular and Plural Forms

Some useful Latin singular and plural forms:

Corpus albicans, corpora albicantia.
Ostium, ostia.
Tendonous cord, chordae tendineae, *or* tendonous cords.
Genitalia *is plural. The term collectively refers to the external organs of genera-tion, namely, the penis, scrotum, and testes in males, and the clitoris, vagina, and labia in females. The singular form has no practical use.*
Lumen, lumina, *or* lumens.
Septum, septa (*not* septae).
Sequel *is English and singular.* Sequela *is Latin and singular.* Sequelae *is plu-ral in both languages. Because many physicians think* sequela *is plural, clear communication might best be served by using* sequel *and* sequelae *for the singular and plural, respectively.*
Vena cava. Venae cavae.

Slang

Slang terms have no place in a typed, signed report. Examples to avoid:

Bleed *as a noun instead of hemorrhage.*
Coded *for cardiac arrest. In formal use, a* code *is a written procedure or pro-tocol used for resuscitation attempts. In slang use,* code *has become synony-mous with the procedures themselves, or the cardiac arrest.*
Full-blown *AIDS for acquired immune deficiency syndrome. "Full-blown AIDS" is an intensive expression; it simply means AIDS. Consider that no one ever has* half-*blown AIDS.*
Raccoon eyes *for spectacle hematomas caused by orbital plate fractures.*
Hinge fracture *for transverse fracture of the base of the skull.*
T-bone *crash for front-to-side vehicular impact.*
Tube *as a verb meaning "to intubate."*

And then there are the terms that have evolved from slang to accepted medical use over the course of a generation:

> *Line* for *catheter*. Only in the field of medicine is the word *line* construed as a linear thing that is hollow. Note that *line* cannot be understood to mean "catheter" unless it is modified by adjectives, whereas *catheter* unambiguously means a hollow tube.

Brand Names

Brand names should be avoided unless the name is stamped on the equipment. Concern with brand names is generally an issue only for the inventory of therapeutic equipment. Few pathologists will be able to keep up with the precise terminology for medical devices. Common examples:

> Foley *catheter. Better:* Urinary catheter.
> Swan-Ganz *catheter. Better:* Pulmonary artery catheter.

General Terminology

Certain casual word usages that would pass unnoticed in oral reports or in handwritten notes in a hospital chart look distinctly unprofessional when appearing in a formal typed report. Numerous examples follow:

> *Adhesed.* There is no such word. The correct word is *adherent.*
> *Alert and oriented.* Some words and phrases are perfectly clear to physicians but can be confusing for laymen. The phrase a*lert and oriented x 1* will be taken by physicians to mean some degree of mental impairment. But a layman encountering this phrase and ignoring the "x 1" could think it simply means alert and oriented. Communication in such a case would be better served by stating that the decedent was lethargic,comatose, or not obeying commands. Or, one could invert the concept and state that the decedent was not oriented to two of three mental status tests.
> *Anthracosis.* This is an important-looking word, but it does not tell the reader whether the lung is that of retired coal miner or a healthy person with the usual carbon deposits outlining the lobules at the visceral pleura. The term should be avoided in favor of more definitive diagnostic terms.
> *Approximately.* When used with a number, does this mean estimated or measured? The better practice is to specify as estimated or measured.
> *Arm.* The term *upper arm* is a lay term for the medical term *arm.* Properly used, the term *arm* refers to the portion of the upper limb that is between the shoulder and the elbow. There is no need to add the word *upper.* The upper extremity comprises the arm, the forearm, and the hand.

Bilateral. In this phrase,

> The bilateral mid-axillary lines

the modifier "bilateral" is unnecessarily redundant to the plural "lines." Nobody speaks this way. Better:

> The mid-axillary lines

Blunt force and *sharp force*. When considered in terms of Newtonian mechanics, these are nonsense terms. The meaning is clear only by convention because the terms are used by so many pathologists. Consider that force can be measured in pounds. There is no such thing as 40 sharp pounds or 40 blunt pounds; force cannot be sharp or blunt. By extension, the terms *sharp force trauma*, *sharp force injury*, and the like are also nonsense terms. However, implements are sharp or blunt, and the corresponding impacts and tissue stress can be said to be sharp or blunt. *Blade wounds* that appear as diagnoses should be termed stab wounds or incised wounds. *Impact wounds* should be called lacerations, fractures, and contusions. *Blunt impact trauma* and *blunt impact wounds* are useful generic terms. Because the corresponding term *sharp impact trauma* is so at odds with customary usage, it does not serve the purpose of communication as well as *blade wounds*. If impact to the head kills by the sole mechanism of cerebral concussion, the term *blunt impact to head* can stand as a diagnosis.

Body can mean the entire set of human remains or merely the trunk. Inasmuch as the gross protocol is presumed to be about the entire set of remains, the more specific *trunk* or *torso* is preferable in most situations where the trunk is being described.

But. The conjunction *but* should be avoided in the descriptive parts of the protocol for the same reason it is useful in good fiction writing: It generates interest because it implies conflict or tension. When used in a protocol, it attracts undue attention from attorneys. The conjunction *and* can be substituted for "but" in most situations.

By and *with*. This is a fine point, but one that is frequently encountered. *By* is the better preposition for passive constructions. *With* is superior for active constructions:

> She poisoned him with arsenic.
> He was poisoned by arsenic.

Inasmuch as death certificates do not name perpetrators, opinions on death certificates use passive constructions; hence,

> Intoxication by heroin

Cardiomegaly is a handy term for radiologists who cannot tell the difference between cardiac *hypertrophy* and cardiac *dilation*. In the hands of a pathologist, *cardiomegaly* is a word that hinders effective communication because it raises a question rather than answering one.

Case. The term *case* should be used with care so as to avoid calling a patient a "case." *Case* is acceptable when describing a lawsuit, a file or folder, or a report.

Chest. The word *chest* is used by modern laymen to refer to the anterior aspect of the thorax, which our 18th-century ancestors called the breast. To physicians who specialize in internal medicine, the chest is the *posterior* aspect of the thorax. The pathologist should make the protocol unambiguous to all readers by using terms such as *anterior aspect of the chest*, or by referencing the anterior or posterior midlines.

Color. The phrase *in color* is almost always useless filler. Stating that *the irides are blue in color* conveys no more information than stating *the irides are blue*.

Consistent with means that the idea is offered as a reasonable medical possibility, not as an opinion to a reasonable degree of medical certainty. A reasonable possibility may fail to rise to the level of more likely than not, because the information needed to reach an opinion is unavailable, or because a lesion is so trivial that an expenditure of investigative effort is unwarranted, as with a skin papule of no importance.

Contain implies the contents of a cavity or lumen:

> The urinary bladder contains 10 ml of clear yellow urine.

However, the aorta does not *contain* atherosclerotic plaques; rather, its walls *have* atherosclerotic plaques. Moreover, if a vital lumen such as that of the trachea contains something, the report should further indicate whether the lumen is *lined* or *occluded*.

Cut surfaces versus *parenchyma*. For solid organs, the pathologist should always describe the cut surfaces. It is possible to describe the liver parenchyma as red-brown by looking through the capsule without ever having dissected the organ. "Cut surfaces" is always plural because there are always at least two cut surfaces. The term *cut sections* is a redundancy. *Cut* and *section* mean the same thing, one in English and one in Latin.

Decedent. The word *decedent* always refers to a previously living person, and never to a dead body. The word is used only in the past tense:

> The decedent was a 64-year-old man with a history of remote myocardial infarction.

But not:

> The decedent has fully developed rigor mortis.

Definitive. This word is usually used to lend an air of precision. When used in a gross protocol, it usually serves the purpose of intensifying the expression. (An example of an intensive expression: *Burned up* is an intensive alternative to *burned* but conveys no additional information.) The problem with an adjective such as "definitive" is that if the report states that there are no definitive ulcers or perforations, it leaves open the possibility of nondefinitive ulcers and perforations. Good practice is to avoid meaningless filler words.

Ecchymosis is a general term for multiple species of blood extravasations. A more specific term is preferred whenever possible. The use of the term *ecchymosis* should be rare outside its use to describe senile ecchymoses on the extremities of the aged.

Evidence. The phrase *no evidence of* can usually be edited down to *no*. For example:

> The leptomeninges have no evidence of meningitis.

provides no more information than

> The leptomeninges have no meningitis.

Expired is an unnecessary euphemism for "died." Options expire. People die. Euphemisms have no place in a scientific report.

Fibrosed. There is no such word. *Are fibrotic* is the usual intended meaning.

Flea-bitten kidney. To the pathologist, this term means little red spots on the surface of the kidney. To the internist, it signifies malignant hypertension. The term has become a buzzword to be avoided.

Fluid. A *fluid* can be a gas or a liquid. Physicians and nurses commonly use the word *fluid* when they mean *liquid*. A well-written report will specify either gas or liquid. However, terms such as *cerebrospinal fluid* are accepted as idiomatic.

Fresh. The term *fresh brain*, as in "the fresh brain weighs 1450 grams," conveys the impression of a delicatessen menu. The term should be avoided.

Glasgow coma "scale" is sometimes misused in place of Glasgow coma *score*. The Glasgow coma scale runs from 3 to 15. The point on the scale occupied by the decedent is the Glasgow coma *score*.

Injury is a legal term that has been borrowed by physicians, and means "not right." As a matter of style, it would seem better to avoid it in conspicuous places like headers. Its primary use is as a synonym for *wound* and *trauma* to create word variety.

Jaw. The word *jaw* by itself can be ambiguous. Physicians generally use the word *jaw* to mean *mandible*. Laymen speak of the upper jaw and the lower jaw. The safest and clearest practice is to use *mandible* and *maxilla*.

Leg. Lower leg is a lay term for *leg*. Properly used, the term *leg* refers to the portion of the lower limb that is between the knee and the ankle. The lower extremity comprises the thigh, the leg, and the foot.

Lesion is from a Latin word for harm. It originally meant wound, but in current medical parlance, it means anything wrong, be it wound or disease. In an autopsy report, about the only use for the word occurs when one cannot classify a finding as a known disease or wound.

Mangled is a word that conveys emotional punch but provides little objective descriptive power. It should not be used as a substitute for a full description of a complicated wound. However, *mangled extremity*, a diagnostic term used by surgeons to refer to an extremity wound that involves some combination of injury to artery, bone, tendon, nerve, or soft tissue, could be used in the opinion section of an autopsy report.

Massive refers to the physical quality of having a large mass. The word nicely describes a cruise ship or a mountain. However, when used by physicians, the word usually signals the cessation of logical thinking and can be translated as "God-awful," "worst I've seen," or "beyond all hope." A well-written report will instead describe a lesion in such a way that the reader can gain a mental picture of the thing being described. *Massive* has no legitimate place in pathological descriptions; the preferred practice is to provide the measured weight or dimensions.

Material. This word makes for weak constructions because it has little information. Its only useful feature is that it is recognizable as a noun. Mucoid *material* could be soot-laden mucus in a bronchus or a well-digested meal sitting in a stomach. The pathologist tempted to use the word *material* should choose another noun that actually conveys information.

Medical intervention might be acceptable as a title for a paragraph because it refers to a process. *Medical intervention* should not be used as a synonym for *medical apparatus*.

Normal. Unremarkable, normal, and *without pathologic change* are all acceptable terms to convey the idea that the pathologist found nothing wrong. Sometimes it more useful to use a pertinent negative expression, and when necessary, to add "except as indicated." For instance, in a body with an endotracheal tube:

> The upper airways have no foreign matter except as indicated.

The designation *normal* can seem silly to some readers who know that the report is describing dead tissue or decomposed organs.

Not dilated is idiomatic. *Nondilated* is bad usage.

Parenchyma is a mass noun, not a count noun. Mass nouns take neither an article nor a plural. Thus,

> The pancreas has pink-tan lobulated parenchyma.

not

> The pancreas has a pink-tan lobulated parenchyma.

Petechial hemorrhage is redundant. All petechiae are hemorrhages by definition.

Penetration and *perforation.* A *perforation* has an entrance and an exit. A *penetration* can be used in a specific sense to indicate that a wound has only an entrance. But the term can also be used in a general sense to indicate any hole. For this reason, *penetrate* is useful in summary constructions that include organs that are perforated and organs that are penetrated, as in

> Gunshot wound to thorax with penetration of aorta, heart, and lung

as a front-sheet diagnosis for a wound that perforates the aorta and lung and grazes the apex of the left ventricle.

Piecemeal necrosis. To the pathologist, it denotes chronic inflammation that has spread out of the portal tracts into periportal hepatic parenchyma, and could represent chronic viral hepatitis, primary biliary cirrhosis, or something else. To the internist, it connotes chronic active hepatitis and nothing else. This phrase has become a buzzword to be avoided.

Resuscitation. The terms *resuscitation attempt* and *resuscitation effort* are usually more appropriate for decedent summaries than the term *resuscitation*, which implies that the decedent actually was revived. The acronym *CPR* is equally undesirable because it implies successful resuscitation.

Remains. As a verb to suggest atrophy, *remains* is not optimal. The statement "A small amount of thymus remains" could suggest that a surgeon or the pathologist has removed a portion of the thymus. *Remnant* should similarly be avoided when the intention is to convey atrophy.

Rupture. Although this word traces its origins to a Latin word meaning "to break," the pathologist can achieve more clarity of style by reserving this term for spontaneous events, and avoiding its use for lacerations. Thus, *rupture* of an aneurysm, *laceration* of the aorta.

Secondary to. Most definitions of the word *secondary* convey some variation on the concept of rank order or the concept of being nonprimary. Its use as a synonym for "caused by" or "because of" should be avoided.

Seizing. Although this verb form is commonly used by medical personnel in casual settings, it is incorrect to state that the patient *is seizing*. There is no active verb for the concept of having a seizure. The reason lies with the etiology of this ancient word. A person who had a seizure was said to have been seized by a demon. So, the demon did the seizing and the patient *had* a seizure. Demons have disappeared from the lexicon of pathogenesis, but seizures have remained.

Shape. In the phrase *triangular in shape*, the phrase *in shape* is redundant and unnecessary.

Sharp force. See "Blunt force."

Significant. In modern usage, *significant* usually conveys the sense of *meaningful* or *important*. The careful pathologist will use this word seldom and only then with forethought as to whether the idea conveyed is that of clinical importance, pathological importance, forensic importance, or legal importance. In autopsy reports, *significant* has most often been used in the negative as a crutch to avoid having to think of how to describe something, to avoid having to describe meaningless minor lesions, or to fend off potential criticism for missing a lesion such as a faint nonsurgical scar:

> The body has no significant surgical scars.

Better:

> The body has no apparent surgical scars.

Status post means that the phrase is going to describe the state of an organ or tissue with reference to a prior event. The term can be useful in a tabular list of diagnoses. For example:

Status post coronary angioplasty 3 Oct 2002: Lumens patent.

If the desired outcome is merely to state that a procedure was performed in the past, and one saw the handiwork, the report should simply list the procedure as if it were a diagnosis. For example,

Endotracheal intubation 3 Oct 2002 to 5 Oct 2002 (anamnestic).

For protocol descriptions, *status post* has no use. One should simply describe what one sees. A prior surgical procedure can be worked into a description without using *status post* as a crutch:

The uterus is absent due to prior remote hysterectomy.

Suggestive of. This phrase is meant to float a trial opinion while denying responsibility for it. In other words, the use of *suggestive of* prevents the reader from knowing whether the pathologist means that the idea that follows the phrase is *speculation*, a *reasonable possibility*, or an *opinion*. See the discussion of parenthetical comments in the section entitled "Inserting Minor Opinions in the Protocol (page 68)."

Superficial abrasion. Almost all abrasions are superficial. Unless it is otherwise stated, a pathologist reading the report will assume that an abrasion is superficial. It is annoying for the informed reader to see all abrasions described as superficial. For the occasional motorcyclist who has abrasions down to the bone, one can describe *deep* abrasions.

Supporting musculature. If there is a supporting musculature, there must be a nonsupporting musculature. The word *supporting* in this context often serves to cover the pathologist's ignorance of the actual names of the muscles. The pathologist can either name the muscles or, when such specificity is unnecessary, refer to them by body region, as in

The wound path runs through the chest wall muscles and perforates the 9th rib.

Toxicity versus *intoxication*. Toxicity is a property that is inherent in a substance independent of the existence of any victim. Intoxication is a property of a victim. *Intoxication* is the term more properly used as a diagnosis.

Transect means "to cut across." *Transection* is best reserved for blade wounds, and avoided when the intended meaning is *complete laceration*.

Trauma is Greek for "wound." Dictionaries state that it has singular and plural (*traumata*) forms, but in common medical use, it is used as a mass noun, like *water*: "This patient has trauma. He has a chest wound and a femoral fracture." Or, an autopsy report might use the word *trauma* in a header but use the word *wound* in the text.

Unresponsive has widespread currency in handwritten medical records. However, it can mean comatose or merely lacking in libido. Specific terms such as *senseless*, *comatose*, and *pulseless* are preferable.

Wall. The terms *chest wall* and *abdominal wall* are commonly understood to mean the muscle and connective tissue (and in the case of the chest wall, ribs) interior to the skin and external to the serosal lining of the body cavity. To describe surface lesions of the skin, the use of the word *wall* can only produce confusion.

Well-developed male genitalia is a phrase to be avoided. *Normally developed* will avoid connotations of size.

Wound is from Old English. In its narrowest sense, it means a mechanical division of tissue, such as a laceration or fracture, but common usage classifies cutaneous wounds as open (lacerations) and closed (abrasions and contusions).

Chapter 5
Death Certification

Purpose and History

A death certificate serves three purposes, described next.

Legal Establishment of Death

The most important of these purposes is the establishment of the fact that the death of a specific person did indeed occur. The largest part of the death certificate is therefore devoted to identifying the decedent by full name, date of birth, place of birth, and names of parents and stating the time and place of death. The identifying data are provided by the funeral director based on interviews with the next-of-kin or other person claiming the remains.

The fact that death occurred and the information about where and when it occurred are usually certified by a physician or medicolegal official (medical examiner or coroner).

Public Health

The second purpose of the death certificate is the collection of data that serve the needs of public health officers. The most important of these data are the medical cause of death and the circumstances of accidental deaths. Depending on the certifying district, other data recorded on the certificate for public health purposes, usually for the purpose of clarifying the stated cause of death, may include the occupation of the deceased, whether smoking or alcohol contributed to death, and whether the deceased was pregnant. These data are provided by the certifying physician or medical examiner.

Disposition of Remains

The third purpose is to record whether the body was buried, cremated, donated to medical science, or removed from the state; and if buried, in what cemetery. These data are provided by the funeral director.

V.I. Adams, *Guidelines for Reports by Autopsy Pathologists*,
© Humana Press, Totowa, NJ 2008

This chapter addresses those aspects of death certification that are performed by a physician or medical examiner.

History

The notion that vital events registration is a state function is a relatively recent idea. For centuries, this task was regarded of ecclesiastical interest only. In England, the established church, first the Roman Catholic Church, and later the Church of England, recorded baptisms (but not births), marriages, and burials (but not deaths). The Colony of Virginia shifted somewhat toward the concept of government responsibility in the early 1600s by collecting notices of christenings, marriages, and burials, but not births or deaths, from Anglican church wardens.

Vital record keeping was first established as a governmental obligation by the Massachusetts Bay Colony in 1639, when the General Court (legislature) passed a law that required each town clerk to record all births, marriages, and deaths. The other New England colonies soon followed suit. Until the 20th century, these clerks recorded vital events with a single handwritten line in a bound journal. The signed certification of death by a physician on a paper form prescribed by the state began early in the 20th century in New England. In states outside New England, the collection of vital records did not begin at all until late in the 19th century.

Death Certificate Forms

Based on recommendations by the World Health Organization, the National Center for Health Statistics develops recommendations for the optimal format for collecting cause-of-death data on death certificates. The individual states of the United States each develop death certificate forms that follow most of these recommendations, but that can vary with respect to collection of data concerning identification and disposition of remains. Some states collect additional data related to cause of death. For instance, the New York State Health Department collects data on natural deaths that occur while operating a motor vehicle. The New York City Health Department (for historical reasons, a data-collecting entity that is distinct from the rest of New York State) collects data on deaths due to complications of medical therapy. The form used by the State of Florida is reproduced as Figure 5.1.

Establishing That Death Occurred

A physician may establish that death occurred by directly witnessing the cessation of vital signs or, if the body was found dead, by determining the absence of vital signs. In many cases, the certifying physician relies on the observations of another physician, a nurse, or paramedics to establish the time of cessation of the heartbeat and respirations.

FLORIDA CERTIFICATE OF DEATH

LOCAL FILE NO.

DEMOGRAPHIC INFORMATION TO BE COMPLETED BY: FUNERAL DIRECTOR

1. DECEDENT'S NAME *(First, Middle, Last, Suffix)*				2. SEX

3. DATE OF BIRTH *(Month, Day, Year)*	4a. AGE-Last Birthday *(Years)*	4b. UNDER 1 YEAR — Months / Days	4c. UNDER 1 DAY — Hours / Minutes	5. DATE OF DEATH *(Month, Day, Year)*

6. SOCIAL SECURITY NUMBER	7. BIRTHPLACE *(City and State or Foreign Country)*	8. COUNTY OF DEATH

9. PLACE OF DEATH *(Check only one)* — HOSPITAL: ___ Inpatient ___ Emergency Room/Outpatient ___ Dead on Arrival
NON-HOSPITAL: ___ Hospice facility ___ Nursing Home/Long Term Care Facility ___ Decedent's Home ___ Other (Specify)

10. FACILITY NAME *(If not institution, give street address)*	11a. CITY, TOWN, OR LOCATION OF DEATH	11b. INSIDE CITY LIMITS? ___ Yes ___ No

12. MARITAL STATUS *(Specify)* ___ Married ___ Married, but Separated ___ Widowed ___ Divorced ___ Never Married	13. SURVIVING SPOUSE'S NAME *(If wife, give maiden name)*

14a. RESIDENCE - STATE	14b. COUNTY	14c. CITY, TOWN, OR LOCATION

14d. STREET ADDRESS	14e. APT. NO.	14f. ZIP CODE	14g. INSIDE CITY LIMITS? ___ Yes ___ No

15a. DECEDENT'S USUAL OCCUPATION *(Indicate type of work done during most of working life.) Do not use "Retired"*	15b. KIND OF BUSINESS/INDUSTRY

16. DECEDENT'S RACE *(Specify the race/races to indicate what decedent considered himself/herself to be. More than one race may be specified.)*
___ White ___ Black or African American ___ American Indian or Alaskan Native *(Specify tribe)*
___ Asian Indian ___ Chinese ___ Filipino ___ Japanese ___ Korean ___ Vietnamese ___ Other Asian *(Specify)*
___ Native Hawaiian ___ Guamanian or Chamorro ___ Samoan ___ Other Pacific Isl. *(Specify)* ___ Other *(Specify)*

17. DECEDENT OF HISPANIC OR HAITIAN ORIGIN? *(Specify if decedent was of Hispanic or Haitian Origin.)* ___ Yes *(If Yes, specify)* ___ No
___ Mexican ___ Puerto Rican ___ Cuban ___ Central/South American
___ Other Hispanic *(Specify)* ___ Haitian

18. DECEDENT'S EDUCATION *(Specify the decedent's highest degree or level of school completed at time of death.)* ___ 8th or less ___ High school but no diploma ___ High school diploma or GED ___ College but no degree ___ College degree *(Specify)*: ___ Associate ___ Bachelor's ___ Master's ___ Doctorate	19. WAS DECEDENT EVER IN U.S. ARMED FORCES? ___ Yes ___ No

20. FATHER'S NAME *(First, Middle, Last, Suffix)*	21. MOTHER'S NAME *(First, Middle, Maiden Surname)*

22a. INFORMANT'S NAME	22b. RELATIONSHIP TO DECEDENT	23a. INFORMANT'S MAILING - STATE

23b. CITY OR TOWN	23c. STREET ADDRESS	23d. ZIP CODE

24. PLACE OF DISPOSITION *(Name of cemetery, crematory, or other place)*	25a. LOCATION - STATE	25b. LOCATION - CITY OR TOWN

26a. METHOD OF DISPOSITION ___ Burial ___ Entombment ___ Cremation ___ Donation ___ Removal from State ___ Other *(Specify)*

26b. IF CREMATION, DONATION OR BURIAL AT SEA, WAS MEDICAL EXAMINER APPROVAL GRANTED? ___ Yes ___ No	27a. LICENSE NUMBER *(of Licensee)*	27b. SIGNATURE OF FUNERAL SERVICE LICENSEE OR PERSON ACTING AS SUCH ▶

28. NAME OF FUNERAL FACILITY	29a. FACILITY'S MAILING - STATE

29b. CITY OR TOWN	29c. STREET ADDRESS	29d. ZIP CODE

MEDICAL CERTIFIER

30. CERTIFIER: *(Check one)*
___ **Certifying Physician** - To the best of my knowledge, death occurred at the time, date and place, and due to the cause(s) and manner stated.
___ **Medical Examiner** - On the basis of examination, and/or investigation, in my opinion, death occurred at the time, date and place, due to the cause(s) and manner stated.

31a. *(Signature and Title of Certifier)* ▶	31b. DATE SIGNED *(mm/dd/yyyy)*	32. TIME OF DEATH *(24 hr.)*	33. MEDICAL EXAMINER'S CASE NUMBER

34a. LICENSE NUMBER *(of Certifier)*	34b. CERTIFIER'S NAME	35. NAME OF ATTENDING PHYSICIAN *(If other than Certifier)*

36a. CERTIFIER'S - STATE	36b. CITY OR TOWN	36c. STREET ADDRESS	36d. ZIP CODE

37. SUBREGISTRAR - Signature and Date ▶	38a. LOCAL REGISTRAR - Signature ▶	38b. DATE FILED BY REGISTRAR *(Mo., Day, Yr.)*

CAUSE OF DEATH TO BE COMPLETED BY: MEDICAL CERTIFIER

39. PROBABLE MANNER OF DEATH ___ Natural	The following are under the jurisdiction of the medical examiner: ___ Accident ___ Suicide ___ Homicide ___ Pending Investigation ___ Undetermined	40. REPORTED TO MEDICAL EXAMINER DUE TO CAUSE OF DEATH? ___ Yes ___ No

41. CAUSE OF DEATH - PART I. *(See instructions on back)* Enter the chain of events - diseases, injuries, or complications - that directly caused the death. Enter only one cause on a line. DO NOT enter terminal event such as cardiac arrest, respiratory arrest, or ventricular fibrillation without showing the etiology. | Approximate Interval: Onset to Death

IMMEDIATE CAUSE (Final disease or condition resulting in death) — a. ____

Sequentially list conditions, if any, leading to the cause listed on line a. Enter the UNDERLYING CAUSE (disease or injury that initiated the events resulting in death) LAST — b. ____ / c. ____ / d. ____

PART II. Other significant conditions contributing to death but not resulting in the underlying cause given in PART I.	42a. WAS AN AUTOPSY PERFORMED? ___ Yes ___ No	42b. WERE AUTOPSY FINDINGS AVAILABLE TO COMPLETE THE CAUSE OF DEATH? ___ Yes ___ No

43a. IF SURGERY MENTIONED IN PART I OR II, ENTER REASON FOR SURGERY	43b. DATE OF SURGERY *(Mo., Day, Yr.)*	44. DID TOBACCO USE CONTRIBUTE TO DEATH? ___ Yes ___ No ___ Probably ___ Unknown

45. IF FEMALE, WAS SHE PREGNANT WITHIN THE PAST YEAR: ___ Yes ___ No ___ Unknown **If Yes, specify timeframe:** ___ at time of death ___ within 1 to 42 days of death ___ within 43 days to 1 year of death

46. DATE OF INJURY *(Month, Day, Year)*	47. TIME OF INJURY *(24 hr.)*	48. INJURY AT WORK? ___ Yes ___ No	49a. LOCATION OF INJURY - STATE

49b. CITY OR TOWN	49c. STREET ADDRESS	49d. APT. NO	49e. ZIP CODE

50. DESCRIBE HOW INJURY OCCURRED	51. PLACE OF INJURY *(e.g. Decedent's home, construction site, restaurant, wooded area)*

IF TRANSPORTATION INJURY, 52a. *Status of Decedent* ___ Driver/Operator ___ Passenger ___ Pedestrian ___ Other *(Specify)*
52b. *Type of Vehicle* ___ Car/Minivan ___ S.U.V. ___ Motorcycle ___ Pickup Truck/Cargo Van ___ Bus ___ Heavy Transport ___ Other *(Specify)*

DH Form 512, Jul. 2004 (Obsoletes previous editions which may not be used)

State of Florida, Department of Health, Vital Statistics

Fig. 5.1 Florida death certificate

Cardiac Death

Historically, the legal definition of death was based on the absence of a heartbeat and respirations. If a body is decomposed or decapitated, the absence of these vital signs is easily inferred by observers with no medical training whatsoever. If a body has been dead for an hour or so, the absence of circulation is readily inferred from the gravitational settling of blood, otherwise known as dependent livor or lividity. This may be ascertained by a layman with minimal medical training. If death has occurred so recently that livor is not apparent, the de-facto contemporary standard requires the demonstration of electrocardiographic silence or cardiac electrical activity that is incompatible with the cardiac output of blood, such as ventricular fibrillation.

Brain Death

In the past several decades, all states have come to recognize the concept of brain death, which permits an individual with a beating heart providing efficient circulation of blood to be pronounced dead if it can be shown that the brain has lost all function. Establishing that brain death has occurred requires sophisticated medical testing by physicians and is always done in a hospital. For the purposes of death certification, the time that brain death is pronounced is the legal time of death. The times that mechanical ventilation is stopped or spontaneous circulation of blood ceases may be of medical interest to organ procurement organizations or autopsy pathologists, but are irrelevant to the purposes of death certification.

Time of Death

The date and time of death recorded on a death certificate can be the date and time that death was witnessed, the date and time that the dead body was found, or the date and time that death was pronounced.

In the case of a body found dead after an interval of being unobserved since the last time known to be alive, the time the body is found dead is recorded. For a body found dead, the certifier need not opine an actual time of death; the time found is adequate for the purposes of death registration. In the rare instances when an opinion of the time of death is required for the purposes of a life insurance company or a probate court, that opinion can be supplied separately at a later date, independent of the death certificate.

When the death occurs in a hospital or nursing home, it is customary to use an administrative time of death when the actual time of cessation of vital signs is unknown or unclear. The administrative time of death, usually known as the time pronounced, may be the time a body is found dead, the time that vital signs ceased, or the time that brain death was established.

Who may pronounce someone dead? In Florida, the statutes are silent on this topic, and the concept of pronouncement of death has no legal meaning for the determination of whether someone is dead by standard criteria. (In contrast, the requirements for determining brain death are quite explicit.) An institution such as a hospital or nursing home may choose to adopt an internal policy that addresses the question of who can pronounce someone dead.

Presumption of Death for a Missing Person

When a person is missing and cannot be located after a diligent search, most states provide for the legal presumption of death after the passage of a certain number of years. For example, in Florida, five years must elapse before such a death is presumed, and the death certificate is signed by a judge. In New York, the period is three years.

Waiting for years for a death certificate can be financially disastrous for the next of kin, because insurance payments are delayed and the settling of estates is delayed. Some state laws permit a judge to make an earlier presumption of death if circumstances clearly and convincingly point to a death. Moreover, some states, including Florida and New York, have laws that state that exposure to a "specific peril of death" is sufficient reason to presume the death of a missing person before the lapse of the prescribed period of time.[1,2]

For example, after the attack on the World Trade Center in 2001, the New York City Attorney's Office, with the help of volunteer lawyers, helped families compile documents that would support a finding that their missing persons were in one of the buildings at the time of the attack. Rather than declare the persons dead, the judge who reviewed the documents declared that there was sufficient information for the medical examiner to provide a death certificate. The medical examiner then issued a death certificate that included the item "body not found." Many certificates were issued within a few weeks of the disaster. If remains were subsequently identified, the death certificates were amended to remove the "not-found" note.[3]

Cause of Death

Codeable Causes of Death

Cause of death is defined in Chapter 2. For the purposes of a death certificate, a cause of death must be expressed with enough etiologic specificity that it can be coded by vital statistics nosologists using the International Classification of Diseases.[4] Because the ICD is also used for clinical and public health purposes, its structure sometimes has more detail than needed by a medical examiner, and sometimes less.

---

[1] §731.103, Florida Statutes and §382.012, Florida Statutes.

[2] New York Consolidated Law Service EPTL §2-1.7 (2006).

[3] Charles S. Hirsch, M.D., personal communication to the author, 23 Nov 2007.

[4] http://www/who.int/classifications/apps/icd/icd10 online.

Chapter	Blocks	Title
I	A00–B99	Certain infectious and parasitic diseases
II	C00–D48	Neoplasms
III	D50–D89	Diseases of the blood and blood-forming organs and certain disorders involving the immune mechanism
IV	E00–E90	Endocrine, nutritional and metabolic diseases
V	F00–F99	Mental and behavioural disorders
VI	G00–G99	Diseases of the nervous system
VII	H00–H59	Diseases of the eye and adnexa
VIII	H60–H95	Diseases of the ear and mastoid process
IX	I00–I99	Diseases of the circulatory system
X	J00–J99	Diseases of the respiratory system
XI	K00–K93	Diseases of the digestive system
XII	L00–L99	Diseases of the skin and subcutaneous tissue
XIII	M00–M99	Diseases of the musculoskeletal system and connective tissue
XIV	N00–N99	Diseases of the genitourinary system
XV	O00–O99	Pregnancy, childbirth and the puerperium
XVI	P00–P96	Certain conditions originating in the perinatal period
XVII	Q00–Q99	Congenital malformations, deformations and chromosomal abnormalities
XVIII	R00–R99	Symptoms, signs and abnormal clinical and laboratory findings, not elsewhere classified
XIX	S00–T98	Injury, poisoning and certain other consequences of external causes
XX	V01–Y98	External causes of morbidity and mortality
XXI	Z00–Z99	Factors influencing health status and contact with health services
XXII	U00–U99	Codes for special purposes

Fig. 5.2 Excerpts from the block list of ICD-10

The chapter list of the ICD lays out the general structure of the coding system (see Figure 5.2). Each chapter or block is indicated by a letter and a range of numerals that begin with 00. For example, Chapter IX covers code blocks I00–I99, which are for disease of the circulatory system (see Figure 5.3).[5] Within Chapter IC, the code I25, for chronic ischemic heart disease, is broken out into a list of four-character codes, using one decimal place, for various forms of chronic ischemic heart disease. As an example of how the ICD structure does not perfectly

I20	Angina pectoris
I21	Acute myocardial infarction
I22	Subsequent myocardial infarction
I23	Certain current complications following acute myocardial infarction
I24	Other acute ischemic heart diseases
I25	Chronic ischemic heart disease

Fig. 5.3 Table of three-character ICD codes for ischemic heart disease. Each of these codes has a subseries of four-character codes

---

[5] Unfortunately, the use of the letters I and O creates the potential for confusion with the numerals 1 and 0.

	Code	Comments
I24.8	Other forms of acute ischemic heart disease, including coronary insufficiency	I24 codes are for acute events that are not infarctions. Ventricular arrhythmias are not mentioned as acute events.
I25.1	Chronic ischemic heart disease: atherosclerotic heart disease [that is to say] coronary artery disease	I25 codes are for chronic manifestations of ischemic heart disease, such as coronary atherosclerosis, old myocardial infarction, aneurysm of heart, and aneurysm of coronary artery.
I25.9	Chronic ischemic heart disease, not otherwise specified	

Fig. 5.4 Possible four-character ICD codes for a death by ventricular fibrillation due to coronary artery disease with no infarction. The code chosen by the nosologist will depend on the wording on the certificate

fit the needs of the medical examiner, sudden death from coronary artery disease, with no infarction and a presumed mechanism of ventricular arrhythmia might be coded in one of three ways, depending on how the certifier words the cause of death (see Figure 5.4).

If the written cause of death is incompetently executed and cannot be coded, the public health purpose of listing the cause of death cannot be served.

In addition to space for the underlying cause of death, the death certificate has room for intermediate and immediate causes of death when a sequence must be laid out. The most important of these is the underlying cause.

A mechanism of death can be listed on the death certificate in place of an immediate cause of death but should be done only for the purpose of clarifying what would otherwise be obscure. Because the vital records nosologists do not code mechanisms, their routine inclusion on death certificates constitutes clutter. Indeed, the small print on most certificates specifically instructs, "Do not enter [a] terminal event such as cardiac arrest, respiratory arrest, or ventricular fibrillation without showing the etiology."

Thus,

Cardiac arrest due to coronary atherosclerosis

is better rendered on the death certificate as

Coronary atherosclerosis (or arteriosclerotic heart disease, atherosclerotic heart disease, ischemic heart disease, or coronary heart disease).

Similarly,

Methicillin-resistant Staphylococcus aureus pneumonia and sepsis

appears to be a competent cause of death. But most cases of bronchopneumonia are the consequence of some underlying condition. The correct underlying cause of death could be leukemia, chronic alcoholism, ischemic heart disease, or any number of conditions. If the underlying cause of death is chronic alcoholism, this should be included. The sepsis can be omitted:

S. aureus bronchopneumonia due to Chronic alcoholism

Similarly,

Metastatic carcinoma of brain

is probably not a competent cause of death, unless the primary site of the cancer was the brain. Vital records nosologists code two elements: malignant tumor and the primary site. Sites of metastases are irrelevant to the purposes of death registration. Better:

Carcinoma of lung metastatic to brain

Even better because there is no way for the nosologist to confuse the primary and secondary sites:

Carcinoma of lung

As mentioned above, the inclusion of the mechanism of death is occasionally useful. The purpose of including a mechanism of death is to achieve clarity:

Cause of death: *Suffocation due to compression of chest.*
How injury occurred: *Car fell off jack while deceased made repairs.*

As mentioned above, a cause of death must be given with enough specificity that a specific ICD code can be selected. Thus, opining

Multiple blunt trauma

as the cause of death in a traffic fatality is inadequate, because it can be coded only as T07 (unspecified injuries). Codeable causes of motor vehicle accident deaths include the following:

Laceration of thoracic aorta due to blunt impact to torso (ICD-10 code S25.0: Injury of thoracic aorta)

and

Fracture of skull base with laceration of brain due to blunt impact to head (code S06.3: Focal brain injury)

Format for Cause-of-Death Opinion

The Rules

The format for capturing the causes of death on the certificates used by most states has two parts. Part I allows only one underlying cause of death but permits its stratification into four levels comprising an immediate cause, two intermediate causes, and one underlying cause. If the certificate is properly executed, the underlying cause is the lowermost line in Part I that has an entry. In other words, the structure of the certificate requires that a chain of causes of death be entered in the reverse of chronological order.

Part II is additionally labeled "Other significant conditions contributing to death but not resulting in the underlying cause given in Part I." Part II does not permit stratification but does permit the inclusion of multiple causes.

Here is an example where this format is used to its fullest capacity, according to the rules:

Part I cause of death:

Bronchopneumonia due to
Congestive heart failure due to
Acute myocardial infarction due to
Arteriosclerotic heart disease

Part II cause of death:

Fracture of femoral neck, diabetes mellitus

Manner and how injury occurred:

Accident (Ground-level fall)

Part II should not be used as a repository for interesting medical curiosities that are not germane to the medical cause of death, as seen in the following example:

Part I:

Carbon monoxide poisoning

Part II:

Focal nodular hyperplasia of liver

Manner of death and how injury occurred:

Suicide (Dec'd ran car in closed garage)

Breaking the Rules

Although the death certificate does not state anywhere that Part I causes of death are to be given more weight than Part II causes, attorneys have been known to work the meaning of "contributing" so as to imply that Part II causes are of minor significance. Therefore, in deaths caused by criminal agency, the certifier with two causes of death to opine, who does not want to give weight to either one, is well advised to put both causes in Part I in violation of the vital records rule against doing so. Thus,

Stab wound of abdomen with penetration of renal vein, and drowning

rather than

Part I. Stab wound of abdomen with penetration of renal vein
Part II. Drowning

Degree of Certainty

In most states, the signature block for the medical examiner includes the following language:

> On the basis of examination and/or investigation, in my opinion, death occurred at the time, date, and place, due to the cause(s) and manner stated.

The death certificate does not state to what level of certainty the cause-of-death opinion must be given. Therefore, unless the medical examiner indicates otherwise, the cause-of-death opinion is to the level of more likely than not.

Contrast the signature block for an attending physician:

> To the best of my knowledge, death occurred at the time, date, and place, and due to the cause(s) and manner stated.

The physician is not required to opine to a level of more likely than not. In the author's view, "best of my knowledge" means "favorite among all possibilities," in other words, best guess.

On occasion, a medical examiner has a cause of death that represents the most likely of all reasonable possibilities and does not rise to the level of more likely than not. If the manner of death is clearly natural, and the medical examiner wants to avoid giving the cause of death as "undetermined" because of its implication that all possible causes are equally likely, he or she can offer the best possibility with the word *probable* appended. Thus, in a case of sudden collapse with no medical history where the examination is limited to an external examination,

> Probable arteriosclerotic heart disease

Used in this way, the word *probable* takes the dictionary meaning of "affording ground for belief" rather than the statistical meaning of "more likely than not."

Approximate Interval: Onset to Death

The death certificates of most states include a column to the right of the spaces for the causes of death permitting the certifier to give a time interval from the onset of the disease to death. This device helps the nosologist sort out a badly framed cause of death. Attending physicians often pay no attention to the sequence demanded by the death certificate form, namely, reverse chronological. The inattentive physician will sometimes write statements such as "Coronary thrombosis due to myocardial infarction due to congestive heart failure."

Experienced medical examiners who write death certificates in the order intended rarely find that the interval column is needed. Occasionally, a registrar of vital records will demand that these spaces be filled. When the medical examiner is confronted with such a demand, the default entry should be *unknown* rather than *years* for most diseases. If *years* is used, the family of the decedent may have trouble collecting insurance benefits because the insurance company will invoke the concept of a pre-existing condition. For example, if a person with no medical history has a sudden death and the autopsy shows coronary artery disease, the most appropriate interval to record, if it is demanded, is "unknown."

Manner of Death

Purpose

Manner of death is defined in Chapter 2. Death certificates have a check-off space to indicate whether the manner of death is natural, accident, suicide, homicide, or undetermined. The manner of death chosen by a medical examiner is not binding on any court, prosecutor, law enforcement agency, or insurance company. Nor is it binding on the state's chief registrar of vital records, who can override and certify any death.

On the death certificate, the manner of death is merely a device to help steer the state vital statistics nosologist toward the correct classification of the cause and circumstances of death. Vital statistics nosologists classify the circumstances of unnatural deaths using the external causation table of the International Classification of Diseases. When pondering what manner of death to select for an unusual set of circumstances, the certifier should consult the structure of the external causation table. In ICD-10, this table is called Chapter XX.

Nevertheless, it is common for police agencies and prosecutors to give some initial weight to the medical examiner's manner of death, and the medical examiner should keep this in mind. Similarly, life insurance companies save money by substituting police and medical examiner investigations for insurance investigations. Life insurance companies are bound only by the language in the insurance policies. However, if the manner of death on the death certificate supports a cheaper insurance settlement, the insurance companies tend to give great deference to the certified manner of death.

In statistical compilations from the National Center for Health Statistics, accident, homicide, and suicide are treated as *causes* of death. This stands in contrast to the practice of medical examiners, for whom the cause and the manner of death are distinct entities.

Natural Deaths

A natural death is one caused exclusively by disease or complications of pregnancy. If a wound or injury caused by external agency contributes to the death in any way, the death is not natural. Natural deaths have no external causation codes.

Suicide

Suicide may be considered first degree self-murder. It requires the demonstration of intent to kill one's self. Intent may be declared in a suicide note or suicidal utterance, or inferred from circumstances, such as enormous drug concentrations in stomach contents. External causation codes for suicide range from X60 to X84.

Accident

An accidental death is one caused by an injury that results from an act of God or from simple negligence without the intent to do harm. For accidents, external causation codes range from V01 to X59 and from Y40 to Y84. These codes include the categories of railway accidents; motor vehicle traffic accidents; motor vehicle nontraffic accidents; water transport accidents; air and space transport accidents; poisoning by drugs, medicinals, and biologicals; poisoning by other solids, liquids, gases, and vapors; misadventures to patients during surgical and medical care; surgical and medical procedures without misadventure; falls; accidents caused by fire and flames; accidents due to environmental factors; accidents by submersion, suffocation, and foreign bodies; and an "other" category that includes accidents caused by machinery, pressure vessels, firearms, explosives, hot substances, electricity, and radiation; and drugs, medicinals, and biological substances in therapeutic use.

Homicide

Homicide is the death of a human at the hands of another person that is not accidental. It includes deaths that are legally classifiable as murder, manslaughter, and excusable or justifiable homicide. Most homicides involve the intent to do harm or some kind of egregious negligence. In the ICD-10, the ICD-9 term *homicide* is replaced by *assault*, the codes range from X85 to Y09 and Y35 to Y36, and they include the categories of injury purposely inflicted, legal intervention (persons killed by police and persons executed for capital crimes), and war wounds.

Undetermined

Deaths that are not classifiable as natural, suicide, accident, or homicide may be classified as undetermined in manner. Classification of a death as being of undetermined manner commonly results from a lack of data. Many such cases involve decomposed bodies, infants whose deaths are otherwise classifiable as sudden infant death syndrome but for whom the circumstances permit no presumption of a natural death, and drug intoxications where there is a suspicion of suicide that does not rise to the level of more likely than not. ICD-10 codes for undetermined manner range from Y10 to Y34.

Manner-of-Death Problems

The manner-of-death definitions given above are not mutually exclusive, and they have logical inconsistencies, perhaps as a result of the concept of manner of death resting on a foundation of blame and intention. Medical examiners disagree frequently on how to assign a manner of death to a specific set of circumstances. Most manner-of-death issues can be resolved by remembering that the manner of death is a mere device to aid the nosologist in selecting the correct code from the external causation table of the International Classification of Diseases. Perusal of the way the table is constructed lends guidance to the following situations.

Motor Vehicle Deaths Where a Driver Leaves the Scene of an Accident

Some medical examiners certify traffic fatalities as homicides if the police file charges against a driver for leaving the scene of an accident. This practice, sometimes ridiculed as opining "postmeditated murder," is incorrect. The manner on the certificate is not binding on the police or the district attorney. There is no incompatibility between an accidental death certificate and a criminal charge of vehicular homicide. Moreover, at the time the death certificate is filed for a traffic fatality, which is usually on the day of the autopsy, one cannot know whether charges might be subsequently filed or dropped. Most importantly, the ICD-10 external causation table clearly places motor vehicle traffic deaths in codes V01 to V89, a section for accidents. The section for homicide (assault) codes has no mention of motor vehicle deaths.

Recreational Drug Abuse

In some quarters, medical examiners assign an undetermined manner of death to ordinary recreational drug intoxication deaths. This practice, which is traceable to the custom in New York City in the 1950s, was predicated on the notion that one could never know for sure when a drug addict meant to commit suicide or had been murdered by having been given a highly concentrated dose of heroin. Here we see speculation elevated to the status of reasonable possibility. If the known circumstances are those of a drug abuser found dead, and do not include any indication of homicidal intent on the part of another person or suicidal intent on the part of the deceased, one is permitted, as a starting point, the rebuttable presumption that the death is accidental.

Russian Roulette and Horseplay with Guns

Russian roulette involves the spinning of the chamber of a revolver-type handgun that contains only one bullet, so that the person holding the revolver has no idea whether the bullet is in the chamber ready to fire. The person holding the revolver then pulls the trigger. One camp of medical examiners calls these deaths accidents based on the theory that Russian roulette is a game of chance, and the victim has no prior expressed suicidal ideation. The other camp, which includes the author, calls these deaths suicides, notes that a handgun has no purpose other than killing people, that with a six-chamber revolver the chance of killing one's self is 16% each time the gun is fired, and that no reasonable person would voluntarily assume a 16% risk of death. The exceptions occur when there is reason to believe that the capacity for reason is diminished, either by gross intoxication or by gross immaturity.

Occasionally, a young child finds a loaded handgun and shoots another child. The medical examiner can opt to opine homicide and let the district attorney find that it is excusable homicide on the part of the surviving child (the part of the owner of the gun is a different matter). Or, the medical examiner can opine accident. The author, using an arbitrary age threshold, opines accident for ages up to 6, and homicide for ages 7 and older.

Firearm Deaths While Hunting Game

In the case of long guns, whose purpose is the hunting of animals for sport, the incidental death of a human at the hands of a hunter who believes he was aiming at game should be classified according to the known circumstances. Most are accidents. If the circumstances are unclear, the death can be classified as undetermined. The ICD has external causation codes for homicidal and suicidal firearm deaths. Accidental firearm deaths are so uncommon that they are classified with a nonspecific external code.

Therapeutic Complications

When a disease progresses to a fatal outcome, it is either by the natural sequelae of the disease or by the sequelae of treatment. If the sequelae of treatment are the expected and usual sequelae, the death is still natural. If the sequelae are unexpected or unusual, one must consider if negligence played a role. If negligence played a role and was egregious, the death can be deemed an accident. If the negligence was ordinary, the death can be deemed natural. In these cases, the nosologist depends heavily on the cause-of-death wording and the wording as to how the injury occurred. When the wording effectively conveys the story, the nosologist does not need to look at the certified manner of death. Therefore, the certifier should select whichever manner seems most in line with the circumstances and disease. For instance, if a patient undergoes a high-risk procedure such as coronary artery bypass for atherosclerosis and has a small air embolus to the brain originating in the left atrium of the heart, the complication may or may not be the result of negligence, and the death is best certified as natural. In contrast, if the surgeon injures the patient because the surgeon is drunk, the negligence is egregious (that is, readily apparent to a non-physician) and the manner can be given as accident.

War Deaths

Occasionally, medical examiners who have a veterans' hospital in their jurisdiction will certify the death of a person who died of complications of a war wound. These deaths are properly called homicides and are given external code Y36.

Deaths by Police

Deaths at the hand of the police, when by firearm, explosive, gas, blunt object, cutting instrument, or other means, are homicides. The ICD-10 external codes for these deaths range from Y35.0 to Y35.4. The concept of "suicide by police," in which a decedent provokes the police into shooting him, has no place in manner-of-death certification. Such circumstances can be set forth in the death certificate item called "How injury occurred."

Death by Execution of Judicial Sentence

Prisoner executions are homicides, classifiable with external code Y35.5.

Fetal Deaths

There is no manner for a fetal death, and fetal death certificates have no provision for including a manner of death.

Compound Manner of Death

The practice of certifying two manners of death at the same time is mentioned only to be condemned. An example is the practice of using the mixed designation "natural-accident" for deaths of elderly persons whose natural disease was triggered into fatal exacerbation by the occurrence of femoral neck fractures. The correct manner of death for these cases is *accident*.

Life Insurance Issues Related to Manner of Death

Typically, life insurance policies exclude payment of a death claim if death is by suicide within some specified period of time after the policy is created (usually one or two years). Full-life policies often pay a double benefit if the death is accidental; these policies, when well-written, usually specify what they mean by an accidental death. Usually, life insurance companies consider a death to be accidental only when it is caused entirely by external causes, and will not pay the double benefit if disease contributed to death in any way.

In the past several years, a cheap form of insurance that pays only for accidental deaths has become popular. As a result, medical examiners have received calls from families asking that a natural death be reformulated as an accidental death. A medical examiner should not opine cause or manner of death in a certain way because it might financially benefit a policy holder. The cause- and manner-of-death opinions should be based only on the circumstances, history, and medical findings.

Circumstances

How Injury Occurred

This section of the death certificate records, in a short sentence or phrase, the circumstances of the injury causing an unnatural death. The information should be sufficient for the nosologist to select the correct external causation code in the International Classification of Diseases. Examples follow.

Traffic Fatalities

The description should include the type of the decedent's vehicle and the types of other objects involved; whether the decedent was the operator or passenger, or a pedestrian; and whether the crash occurred in the right-of-way or off the road. The example

> Unhelmeted motorcyclist

is insufficient because it lacks the other part of the collision. It can be coded only as V29 (motorcycle rider in unspecified transport accident). The example is wordy because the helmet status is not codeable. Better, because it has a specific code (V23.4, motorcycle driver in collision with car, pick-up truck or van, in traffic):

> Motorcyclist in collision with van

Similarly,

> Driver vs. steering wheel

does not convey the needed information, and can be coded only as V49, car occupant in unspecified transport accident. Furthermore, this statement has unneeded information: The nosologists do not care about internal collisions in the cabin. Better, and coded as V47.5 (car driver in collision with fixed object, in traffic):

> Driver of automobile, left road, struck tree

The following, if the place of injury is a driveway rather than a public road, would meet the needs of the nosologists, who would code it as V03 (pedestrian injured in collision with car, pick-up truck, or van, not in traffic):

> Pedestrian run over by rolling automobile

Falls

The description of a fall must include whether the fall involved ice and snow (W00), slipping, tripping, or stumbling on the same level (W01), a wheelchair (W05), a bed (W06), a chair (W07), or any of several other circumstances including stairs, a ladder, and the like.

Firearm Deaths

For a death by firearms, the description of how the injury occurred must indicate whether the firearm was a handgun, was a long gun, or cannot be specified. For example:

> Shot self with shotgun (X73)

Submersion

For deaths by submersion, the certifier must indicate whether the circumstances involved a swimming pool (W67), a swimming pool because of a fall (W68), natural water (W69), natural water because of a fall (W70), and the like. Example for a toddler:

Entered in-ground swimming pool and submerged unobserved by caretaker

Drug Abuse

Recreational drug abuse deaths can be described very simply. In most cases, the route of entry of the drug is unknown and does not need to be specified. As long as the cause of death specifies the type of drug or drugs, the circumstances can be given simply as

Drug abuse

External causation coding requires enough information to indicate whether the intoxication was by narcotics, sedatives, or other drug groups. This is most efficiently conveyed by the cause-of-death entry.

Specifying drug abuse as *chronic* in the absence of a history of prior drug use may lead to a phone call from an irate parent asserting that the child had never used drugs before the fatal event. The modifier *chronic* is unnecessary.

Location of Injury

The location of injury is the physical address where the injury occurred: street, city, and state.

Place of Injury

The place of injury is a description of the site, suitable for statistical compilation. Examples:

Decedent's home
Public road
Suspension bridge
Body of fresh water

The external causation table (Chapter XX of the ICD-10) includes a table of places that is used by the nosologists to code places for some unnatural deaths. Perusal of this table will afford the certifier an idea of how much detail is required in the place-of-injury entry:

Place code "0," for home, is the code used whenever the place is given on the certificate as apartment, boarding house, trailer park, farmhouse, home, house, any kind of non-institutional place of residence, the yard, driveway, garage, or garden of a home, or a private swimming pool.

Place code "1" is for any kind of residential institution and includes children's home, dormitory, hospice, military camp, nursing home, old people's home, orphanage, prison, or reform school.

Place code "2" is for school, other institution, or public administrative area. It includes assembly hall, campus, church, college, hospital, library, and many others.

Place code "3" is for sports and athletic areas and includes athletic fields, courts, and stadiums as well as public swimming pools.

Place code "4" is for public roads of all kinds.

Place code "5" is for trade and service areas and includes airports, banks, hotels, shopping malls, and bus stations.

Place code "6" is for industrial areas and construction sites.

Place code "7" is for farms and ranches.

Place code "8" is for other specified places, including railroad lines and military training grounds. Many of the examples given by the ICD-10 are natural outdoor areas.

Place code "9" is for unspecified places.

For the four examples given at the beginning of this section, the resulting place codes would be 0, 4, 8, and 8, respectively.

Chapter 6
Record Retention

Purpose

By temperament, physicians are generally well suited to working up one patient at a time and creating records of the resulting investigations. Nothing in a physician's training prepares him or her for the task of managing an inventory of paper records or physical evidence.

Contrast the registrar of vital records, or the register of deeds. Both are focused on maintaining records in perpetuity and making them accessible through indexes. They do not create the records of which they are custodians. Vital records are meant to be available for centuries, to serve the needs of public health research and those of historians. Likewise, the existence of reliable repositories for copies of property deeds is fundamental to the preservation of property rights.

The useful lifespan of most government records, unlike that of property deeds, is considerably less than perpetuity.

A record retention schedule is a device for managing an inventory of paper records by organized disposal. The fundamental concept is that because not all records are of equal value over time, records can be discarded when they no longer serve a purpose. All large government offices have record retention schedules and use them to discard unneeded records in an orderly fashion.

If records are discarded in a random manner or simply lost, then a suspicion could arise that some record was discarded in order to hide an act of malfeasance. Alternatively, when records are retained forever, some attrition is inevitable for a variety of reasons. These reasons can include the sending of an original report instead of a copy, misfiling in the wrong case folder (misfiling is much worse than having a backlog of unfiled papers), and retention by a pathologist for study or research.

The following section draws extensively on the retention schedule developed by the Florida Secretary of State for medical examiner records.[1] Other states may have different requirements for medical examiners or no requirements at all. If a state has

---

[1] Florida Department of State, General Records Schedule GS2: Law enforcement, correctional facilities, and district medical examiners. Available on the Internet at http://dlis.dos.state.fl.us/recordsmgmt/gen_records_schedules.cfm.

V.I. Adams, *Guidelines for Reports by Autopsy Pathologists*,
© Humana Press, Totowa, NJ 2008

no requirements for record retention that are specific to medical examiner records, the medical examiner should develop, pursuant to existing state law, office-specific policies that accomplish the same thing.

Generally, a retention schedule specifies that a particular type of record is to be retained until one of the following occurs:

A fixed interval of time passes.
An event occurs that converts the record to another type of record.
The record becomes obsolete or superseded, or its administrative value is lost.

The concept of a record that must be kept in perpetuity is alien to record retention experts.

Types of Records

Autopsy Reports

In Florida, a medical examiner autopsy report or any other signed report on a body that has been identified must be retained for 30 years. The medical examiner may retain the report for longer than 30 years at his or her discretion. An autopsy report on a body that has not been identified must be retained until the body has been identified. If the body is never identified, the report is held in perpetuity.

Case File Notes

All the findings, reports of radiographs, opinions, laboratory test results, photographs, and case notes for a death in which the medical examiner provided the death certificate are held for at least 30 years if the body has been identified. If the body has not been identified, these records are held until the body has been identified.

Death Certificates

The vital records office of the state is the custodian of death certificates. Copies of partially completed death certificates in the medical examiner file may be discarded when they are superseded or their administrative value is lost. They are superseded when a final certificate is registered by the vital records office. Whether these copies have administrative value beyond the date that a final certificate is registered by the vital records office depends on the needs of the medical examiner. If there is no other record of when a death certificate was initially signed or finally signed after waiting for further investigation, then the copy may be considered to have administrative value. The author retains copies of partially completed certificates for the life of the case folder.

Deposition Transcripts

In states such as Florida where attorneys in criminal cases have the right to take depositions from witnesses, the medical examiner files for homicides may have copies of deposition transcripts. Although the originals are in the custody of the clerk of courts, and copies may usually be had through the prosecutor's office, these copies are usually retained by the medical examiner as a convenience. The administrative value lies in the convenience.

Police Reports

Theoretically, copies of police reports should be redundant to the originals on file with the law enforcement agency. However, experience has shown that police agencies, with their vastly larger number of case files, often cannot find reports of interest to the medical examiner, especially after the lapse of some years. Retention of these reports by the medical examiner is an administrative convenience at the discretion of the medical examiner.

Hospital Patient Records

Medical examiners frequently receive photocopies of hospital records of decedents. Because these are copies, not the original records, the applicable retention period is "until obsolete, superseded or administrative value is lost." This means that the hospital records can be discarded when the medical examiner has no further use for them. In the author's office, these duplicate hospital records are discarded immediately after the autopsy report is signed. This is possible because of an office policy that, for all deaths in hospitals, requires the medical examiner to create a written synopsis of the hospital course. This summary is perfectly sufficient to prepare for later testimony in criminal cases. In civil cases, if the record needs to be consulted again, the attorney requesting the consultation or deposition will gladly provide a fresh copy of the record, usually sorted, tabbed, and organized better than the copy originally read by the medical examiner.

Autopsy Recordings

Voice recordings of an autopsy, including dictation tapes, are retained only until the verbatim transcription has been verified by the medical examiner. They may, of course, be retained longer. The rationale is that the tapes serve no public purpose once the report has been transcribed and signed. The fact that the preservation of such tapes may serve the private purposes of an attorney who is looking for grist for the mill of cross-examination is of no import to the public purposes of the retention schedule.

Investigations of Bodies to Be Cremated

In several states, the medical examiner is required to investigate a death when the body is to be cremated, independent of the cause or manner of death. Records from these investigations usually consist of faxed copies of death certificates signed by attending physicians. In Florida, the actual death certificate held by the Health Department serves as the primary record. The medical examiner's faxed copy may be discarded when its administrative value is lost (that is, when the medical examiner determines that no further investigation is required). Other file notes related to this type of activity must be retained for four years. In the author's office, these file notes are maintained in electronic form only.

No-Jurisdiction Case Notes

When a death is referred to the medical examiner and a determination is made that the medical examiner has no jurisdiction and no further investigation is required, the resulting notes are retained for four years. In the author's office, the notes are retained in electronic form only.

Business Records

Employment records, time sheets, receipt books, budget records, and the like typically have retention schedules specified by state law, and are not covered here. Typical times for these sorts of records in Florida are on the order of four years or so. Some employment record retention schedules are specified by federal law.

Physical Evidence

Radiographs

X-ray films are considered physical evidence in Florida, not records. Their retention is governed by state administrative code.

Paraffin Blocks and Histological Slides

Paraffin blocks and histological slides are considered physical evidence in Florida, not records. Their retention is governed by state administrative code. Both are required to be retained for a minimum of 10 years.

Appendix 1: Autopsy Protocol in Case of Gunshot Wounds and Intoxication

HILLSBOROUGH COUNTY, FLORIDA

MEDICAL EXAMINER DEPARTMENT[1]
401 SOUTH MORGAN STREET
TAMPA, FLORIDA 33602
813-272-5342

Report of Diagnosis and Autopsy

on

[name of decedent]

File 0x − 0xxxx

---

[1] The county seal, contact information, decedent name and case number were brought out to a title page in order to provide more room on the diagnosis page.

OPINION

Final Diagnosis:

Gunshot wound to chest, penetrating,[2] indeterminate range.
    Perforation of heart and lungs.
    Pericardial and pleural hemorrhage[3] Gunshot wound to left thigh, perforating, indeterminate range.
    Intoxication[4] by ethyl alcohol

Cause of Death:

Gunshot Wound to Chest, with Perforation of Heart and Lungs

Manner of Death:

Homicide (Shot by other person with handgun)

                        [name of pathologist], M.D.   Date Signed
                        Associate Medical Examiner

---

[2] From the word "penetrating," the reader can know that there is a bullet.

[3] The more dynamic form, "pleural hemorrhage" is chosen over that static form, "hemothorax."

[4] "Intoxication" is an opinion that is independent of morphologic findings.

Death: [date] at 0104 hours	*Autopsy:* [date]
[street address]	401 S Morgan St, Tampa
Age: 23 years	*Performed by:*
Length and Weight: 5'05", 124 pounds	[name of pathologist], M.D.

DESCRIPTION OF AUTOPSY FINDINGS

Clothing:

The body is received clothed in a white sleeveless T-shirt, black running pants, blue bikini underwear and blue and black flip-flops sandals. A gunshot defect is in the left pectoral region of the T-shirt, with no soot or gunpowder on the surrounding fabric.

External Examination: 28 May 2003 at 1255 hours

The body is that of a well-developed, well-nourished man who appears consistent with the above-stated length, weight, and age. The body length is personally measured at 65". Rigor mortis is fully developed. Livor mortis is posterior, partially blanches with digital pressure, and extends to the posterior axillary line. The body is cold from refrigeration. The anterior aspect of the left shoulder has a few small postmortem tan-yellow ant bites.

The scalp is atraumatic and is covered by straight black hair in a full distribution. The skin is light brown. The irides are brown and the pupils are midsized.[5] The conjunctivae have no petechiae. Facial hair comprises a mustache and chin whiskers. The nasal septum is intact. The oral mucosa has no injuries. The teeth are natural and in fair repair.

The neck, back, chest, and abdomen have no masses or scars. The penis is uncircumcised and free of injuries. The testes are descended. The anus has no injuries. Adhesive cardiac monitors on are on torso.[6]

The upper and lower extremities have no masses. The lateral aspect of the right shoulder has a tattoo of a heart and an illegible word.

---

[5] The decedent was ethnically Hispanic. No attempt to assign a race is made here. Rather, a few physical features are described.

[6] Because the medical devices occupy only a single sentence, a special paragraph for medical devices and artifacts is not needed.

Gunshot Wound of Chest[7]:

1. An entrance gunshot wound is in the left pectoral region of the chest, medial and superior to the left nipple, 14 1/2″ inferior to the top of the head, 50 1/2″ superior to the sole of the left foot, and 2 1/4″ left of the anterior midline. The wound, including the abrasion collar, is round and 0.8 cm in diameter. The abrasion collar is circumferential, regular, and slightly wider along the lateral aspect. No soot deposition or gunpowder stippling is on the skin or in the soft tissues around this wound.

2. The wound path sequentially runs through the left third intercostal space anteriorly, the anterior portion of the upper lobe of the left lung, the pericardial sac, the heart, the lower lobe of the right lung, and the right 8th intercostal space posteriorly, to end in the subcutaneous tissue on the right side of the back. The path through the heart is described in further detail[8]:

    The path through the heart begins as a circular perforation on the anterior aspect of the right ventricular outflow tract, then continues as a perforation of the base of the heart at the root of the aorta and pulmonary artery, and then passes through the posterior portion of the atrial septum. It leaves the heart at the origin of the right inferior pulmonary vein.

3. Recovered from the end of the wound path is a moderately deformed, non-jacketed, small-caliber lead bullet, located on the right side of the back 47″ superior to the sole of the right foot, and 4 1/2″ right of the posterior midline. The bullet is left uninscribed, and is photographed on a labeled evidence envelope before being sealed in the envelope.

4. Associated findings comprise extravasation of blood into tissue along the wound pathway, a measured 400 milliliters of blood in the right pleural cavity, a measured 100 milliliters of blood in the pericardial sac, and a measured 1 liter of blood in the left pleural cavity. The hemothoraces are associated with partial collapse of both lungs.

5. The direction of the wound path, with respect to the standard anatomic position, is left to right, front to back, and downward.

Gunshot Wound of Left Thigh:

1. The entrance wound is on the anterior aspect of the left thigh proximally, just inferior to the left groin fold, 34″ inferior to the top of the head, 31″ superior to the sole of the left foot, and 3 1/4″ left of the anterior midline. The wound, including the abrasion collar,[9] is round and 0.6 cm in diameter. The enclosed entrance perforation is 0.4 cm in diameter. The abrasion collar is thin, crescen-

---

[7] Most of the paragraphs in this section begin with a key word or phrase that indicates what the paragraph is about.

[8] The pathologist has opted to use two paragraphs for the wound path. The first names all the organs perforated. The second gives detail that would be of interest only to a physician.

[9] The pathologist has chosen to take the outside dimensions of the abrasion collar as the main measurement.

tic, and is at the superior edge of the wound from 11 to 1 o'clock. No soot deposition or gunpowder stippling is on the skin or in the soft tissues around this wound.

2. The wound path runs through the musculature of the anterior and lateral aspects of the left thigh, without perforation of the neurovascular structures, to exit at the lateral aspect of the thigh. There is no bullet. Blood is extravasated into the tissues along the wound pathway.[10]

3. The exit perforation is on the lateral aspect of the thigh, 30″ superior to the sole of the left foot. It is a 0.5×0.3 cm perforation with no marginal abrasion and no apparent tissue deficit.

4. The direction of the wound path, with respect to the standard anatomic position, is right to left, front to back, and downward.

Blunt Impact Wounds:

1. The left eyebrow laterally has a 0.8 centimeter in-greatest-dimension purple contusion.

2. The upper central portion of the back has a 0.9 centimeter in-greatest-dimension red-brown abrasion.

3. The left shoulder laterally has a 2×0.7 centimeter red-brown abrasion.

4. The left elbow laterally has a 2×1.5 centimeter red-brown abrasion.

5. The left wrist dorsally has two punctate red-brown abrasions.

6. The left shin anteriorly has two pink contusions measuring 1.0 and 1.6 centimeters.

Internal Examination[11]: 28 May 2003 at 1330 hours

Head: The scalp, skull, and meninges have no injuries. The epidural and subdural spaces have no liquid accumulations. The brain weighs 1350 grams. It has translucent leptomeninges and clear cerebrospinal fluid. The hemispheres are symmetric. The cranial nerves, cerebral arteries, and external and cut surfaces of the brain are unremarkable.

Neck: The strap muscles, hyoid bone, and laryngeal cartilages have no injuries. The tongue has no bite marks or contusions. The pharynx, larynx, and trachea have smooth mucosal linings, without masses or obstruction.

Body Cavities: The pneumothorax test is negative bilaterally. The pericardial, pleural, and peritoneal cavities have smooth linings. The peritoneal cavity contains no blood or excess liquid.[12] The viscera are normally situated, are generally pale, and have no abnormal odors.

---

[10] Because this was the only item that would be suitable for a separate paragraph of associated findings, the item was conveniently placed here.

[11] The internal findings pertinent to the wounds have all been described in the special wound sections and are not repeated here.

[12] The pericardial and pleural cavity contents have already been described.

Cardiovascular: The heart weighs 270 grams. It has a smooth epicardial surface. The coronary ostia arise normally from the sinuses of Valsalva. The epicardial coronary arteries have normal distributions. The posterior descending artery arises from the right coronary artery.[13] The arteries are patent and of normal caliber. The cardiac chambers are neither hypertrophied nor dilated. The atrial and ventricular septa are intact, with the exception of the bullet perforation of the atrial septum. The myocardial cut surfaces are red-brown and have no infarcts. The endocardial surfaces are smooth. The aortic and pulmonic valve cusps are disrupted by the gunshot wound described above, but the valve cusps and leaflets are otherwise unremark able.

The great vessels connect to the heart in a normal fashion and are empty of blood.[14] The great vessels contain no thrombi. The aortic arch has a normal branching pattern. The aorta has a smooth tan intima, with minimal atherosclerotic streaks. *Pulmonary:* The right and left lungs weigh 280 and 200 grams, respectively. The pleural surfaces are smooth. The cut surfaces are red-pink and crepitant, with the exception of hemorrhagic areas along the aforementioned gunshot wounds. The lungs have no masses or granulomas. The tracheobronchial tree is unobstructed. The pulmonary vessels are unremarkable.
Digestive: The esophagus, stomach, and small and large intestines have no masses or obstructions. The stomach contains a measured 500 milliliters of tan liquid with fragments of partially digested food. The stomach and duodenum have no ulcers or erosions.
Liver, Gallbladder, and Pancreas: The liver weighs 1200 grams. It has a smooth capsular surface and tan parenchyma, without masses or cysts. The hepatic veins are patent. The hepatoduodenal ligament has no fibrosis. The gallbladder contains a measured 15 milliliters of olive-yellow bile, without gallstones. The extrahepatic bile ducts are patent. The pancreas has lobulated tan parenchyma, with no masses or calcifications.
Hemic and Lymphatic: The spleen weighs 70 grams. It has a smooth capsular surface and red-purple parenchyma, without masses. The vertebral bone marrow is red-brown. The lymph nodes and palatine tonsils are not enlarged. The thymus has lobulated tan parenchyma, which is partially effaced by fat.
Endocrine: The pituitary gland is normal in size and has no masses. The thyroid gland has pink parenchyma, without nodules. The adrenal glands have thin yellow cortices and gray medullae, without masses or hemorrhages.
Genitourinary: The right and left kidneys weigh 80 and 100 grams, respectively. The cortical surfaces are smooth. The corticomedullary demarcations are sharp. The kidneys have no masses or cysts. The collecting systems are not dilated. The urinary bladder has a smooth white mucosa and contains a measured 15 milliliters of

---

[13] Rather than opine a left or right dominant coronary distribution, the pathologist has chosen to give the anatomic findings that would support such an opinion.

[14] For the purpose of estimating the percent of total blood volume lost, describing the content and degree of filling of the great vessels is more important and more reliable than estimating the volume of external blood loss at a scene.

cloudy yellow urine. The prostate gland has rubbery tan-white parenchyma, without masses. The seminal vesicles are unremarkable. The testes have white tunics and tan parenchyma, without masses or contusions.

Musculoskeletal: The musculature is firm, red-brown, and normally developed. The bony consistency is normal. The clavicles, sternum, spine, ribs, and pelvis have no recent fractures.

NOP:del   06/05/03

MICROSCOPIC DESCRIPTION

Heart, Left Ventricle: Mild nuclear changes of hypertrophy.
Lung: Unremarkable except for patchy atelectasis.
Liver: Unremarkable.

[transcriptionist and date]

— End of Autopsy Report; Toxicology Report is Appended —

Appendix 2: Autopsy Protocol in Case of Impact Wounds and Natural Disease

HILLSBOROUGH COUNTY, FLORIDA

MEDICAL EXAMINER DEPARTMENT
401 SOUTH MORGAN STREET
TAMPA, FLORIDA 33602

813-272-5342

Report of Diagnosis and Autopsy[1]

on

[name of decedent]

File 0x − 0xxxx

---

[1] The use of both "diagnosis" and "autopsy" underscores the fact that the report has a subjective part and an objective part.

Opinion

Final Diagnosis:

Blunt impact to head[2]
 Fractures of vault and base of skull
 Lacerations of dura mater
 Lacerations of brainstem and cerebrum
Blunt impact to torso
 Fracture of left clavicle
 Fractures of left ribs
 Laceration left leaf of diaphragm with
  pleural herniation of spleen and stomach
 Lacerations of liver, spleen, mesenteries,
  and gallbladder
Blunt impacts to extremities
 Laceration of right hip penetrating muscle
 Fracture right femur
 Open fracture of left ankle
Chronic alcoholism[3]
 Cirrhosis and fatty change of liver
Cholelithiasis and chronic cholecystitis
Hypertensive heart disease

Cause of Death:

Fractures of Skull Base and Lacerations of Brainstem *due to*
Blunt Impact to Head

Manner of Death:

Accident (Motorcyclist in collision with pickup truck[4])

———————————————————————
 [name of pathologist], M.D.   Date Signed
 Medical Examiner

---

[2] In addition to the diagnoses that are largely morphologic, the opinion page, or front sheet, can include diagnoses that are based on the totality of known information. The impact to the head was not seen by the pathologist; it was inferred from the morphological findings and the known circumstances.

[3] The diagnosis of alcoholism is based on the social and medical history.

[4] The parenthetical inclusion of the circumstances, as they appear on the death certificate, is more important to the formation of the diagnoses listed above than is the inclusion of "accident" as the manner of death.

Death: [date] at 2328 hours
[street address]
Age: 47 years
Length and Weight: 5′ 11″, 181 pounds

Autopsy: [date]
401 S Morgan St, Tampa
Performed by[5]:
[name of pathologist], M.D.

Description of Autopsy Findings

External Examination: 28 August 2005 at 0915 hours

The body is that of an adult man appearing the above-stated age, length, and weight[6]. Body build is medium. Rigor mortis is fully developed. Lividity is posterior, purple, minimally developed, and partly fixed. The torso is cold from refrigeration.

The scalp hair is 1/8″ long and brown. The irides are brown. The conjunctivae have no petechiae. The face is clean-shaven. The teeth are natural and are in good repair. A clear plastic orthodontic device covers the maxillary teeth. The external genitalia are those of a normally developed circumcised adult male. The pubic hair at the base of the penis has been recently shaved. The chest has a barrel shape. The left side of the chest anteriorly has a depression corresponding to rib fractures described presently. The anus is unremarkable. The body has no ankle edema, no tattoos, no apparent surgical scars, and no recent injuries except as indicated.

Blunt Impact Wounds—External and Internal:
Head and Neck:

1. The forehead, the top of the head, and the back of the head have large abrasions. The nose is abraded[7].
2. The vault and base of the skull have multiple fractures, many of which are displaced. Beginning from the right occipital area in the region of the external occipital protuberance, fractures radiate into the vault, around the left side toward the region of the upper ear, and then toward the vertex and the frontal area, with multiple branches radiating from a principal fracture line.[8] The base

---

[5] Had the autopsy been performed by one pathologist and signed off by another (e.g., if the pathologist who performed the autopsy had become unavailable), the name appearing here would differ from that on the front sheet.

[6] If the length and weight are measured by an assistant, these measurements are best placed outside the text dictated by the pathologist.

[7] The numbering of the wound paragraphs serves mainly to give the wound section a distinctive look.

[8] Curiously, the more detailed the description of skull fractures, the more confusing. A sketch on a skull diagram is particularly helpful as part of the case file.

of the skull has a transverse fracture line through the roofs of the middle ears and the body of the sphenoid bone. Other fracture lines involve the posterior fossa, leaving the petrous ridges mobile. Some of these fracture lines intersect with the foramen magnum. The dura mater at the base of the skull is multiply lacerated. A few fracture lines involve the middle and anterior fossae. The fractures are all somewhat displaced.

3. The brain[9] has multiple lacerations as follows: The midbrain is 3/4 lacerated and is also stretched. The pontomedullary junction is entirely lacerated. The spinomedullary junction is 90% lacerated. The arachnoid mater is torn open in the region of the Sylvian fissures and the optic chiasm. Thin subarachnoid hemorrhages are over the cerebral and cerebellar hemispheres. No spinal fluid remains. The cerebral ventricles are lined by thin red liquid. The corpus callosum and the septum pellucidum are lacerated. The inferior surfaces of the temporal lobes have small lacerations.

Torso:

1. The upper abdomen and right costal regions of the torso have small cutaneous[10] abrasions. The left hip anterolaterally over the iliac crest has a medium-size abrasion. The skin over the left shoulder blade has multiple medium-size abrasions. The small of the back on the left side has a large abrasion. The right side of the small of the back has a large contusion within which are small abrasions. The right hip posterolaterally has a $7 \times 1 \times 5\,cm$ deep laceration with widely abraded margins; the abrasions extend onto the right buttock. The laceration undermines widely in all directions, penetrates to muscle and bone, and extends past the greater trochanter of the femur to a maximum depth of $5\,cm$. The buttocks[11] are contused medially.

2. The left clavicle has a complete fracture of the shaft. The adjacent fat at the base of the neck has extravasated blood. The junction of the right clavicle, the right sternocleidomastoid muscle, and the fat of the posterior triangle at the base of the neck on the right side has a small focus of extravasated blood.

3. Left ribs two through eight are serially fractured with moderate displacement and with several parietal pleural lacerations.[12] Blood extravasation into the soft tissues is minimal. The thoracic portion of the vertebral column has a chip fracture of one of the bodies in the lower thoracic portion with laceration of the

---

[9] The name of the organ appears early in the paragraph and helps to orient the lay reader to the descriptions that follow.

[10] When the description shifts from the internal wounds of the head to the external wounds of the torso, it is helpful to reorient the read to the organ, namely, skin.

[11] Notice that the placement of the anatomical location at the beginning of each sentence makes it easier to locate a particular wound.

[12] Noting serosal lacerations is useful. It can explain bloody effusions in a cavity. Further, a fractured rib will not lacerate the lung unless the pleura is torn.

anterior longitudinal ligament. The posterior and lateral elements are palpably intact and cannot be dislocated.

4. The left leaf of the diaphragm has a 20 cm long laceration where the leaf meets the chest wall laterally. Through this laceration the spleen and the stomach are herniated into the left pleural cavity.
5. The left pleural cavity has a measured 1300 milliliters of thin red liquid. The right pleural cavity has a measured 50 milliliters of thin red liquid.[13] The peritoneal cavity has an estimated 50 milliliters of thin red liquid.
6. The spleen has a 7 cm long laceration, the thickness of which is limited to the capsule.
7. The liver has several shallow capsular lacerations that penetrate only a few millimeters into the parenchyma.
8. The falciform ligament is partly torn off the abdominal wall.
9. The sigmoid mesocolon and the mesentery of the small bowel have several penetrating lacerations.
10. The anterior aspect of the gallbladder has a 2 cm full-thickness laceration.

Extremities:

1. The left upper extremity has a small cutaneous abrasion of the dorsal aspect of the forearm near the elbow. The back of the left hand has a small abrasion.
2. The right upper extremity has a closed fracture of the shaft of the humerus. The posterior aspect of the right arm has a small abrasion and a medium-sized contusion near the elbow. The dorsal aspect of the right wrist has a small abrasion. The dorsal aspect of the third finger of the right hand has a transversely oriented $1 \times 0.1 \times 0.2$ cm deep cutaneous laceration that penetrates to the periosteum.[14]
3. The left lower extremity has an open fracture-dislocation of the ankle anteriorly. The cutaneous laceration is 15×10 cm and the wound is 2 cm deep. The cutaneous margins are abraded and several foot bones are exposed. The skin around the left kneecap has a cluster of small abrasions. The left leg along the medial aspect of the shin has a vertically oriented, medium-sized, cutaneous abrasion.
4. The right lower extremity has a closed fracture of the shaft of the femur. The skin near the right knee has a cluster of small abrasions and contusions anteromedially. The right foot has multiple abrasions and contusions of the medial aspect.

Having been described, the injuries will not be repeated.

Internal Examination: 28 August 2005 at 0915 hours

Head: The scalp, skull, and meninges have no injuries except as described above. The epidural and subdural spaces have no blood. The brain weighs 1560 grams. The

---

[13] The volume of serous effusions and pus can be estimated, but the volume of blood should be measured, in order to estimate total blood loss.

[14] Lacerations should be measured in three dimensions or, if trivial, in one greatest dimension, labeled as such.

cranial nerves and cerebral arteries are unremarkable. The external and cut surfaces of the brain are remarkable only as indicated above.

Neck: The cervical spine, the laryngeal cartilages, and the hyoid bone have no fractures. The prevertebral fascia has no blood. The tongue has no contusions. The upper airways have thin streaks of bloody mucus.

Body Cavities: The body cavities have liquid accumulations as described above. The pleural window test is negative bilaterally. The hepatorenal recess of the peritoneal cavity on the right has multiple 1 to 2 mm dark green concretions (Comment: from the lacerated gallbladder).[15] The organs, with the exceptions indicated above, are normally situated. They have minimal congestion and are somewhat wet.

Cardiovascular: The aorta has a few orange fibrolipid atherosclerotic plaques occupying no more than 5% of the intimal surface area.[16] The venae cavae have no thrombi. The pulmonary trunk and arteries have no thromboemboli. The great vessels and the chambers of the heart are entirely collapsed and contain no recoverable blood.

The heart weighs 440 grams (Comment: The expected heart weight is 360 grams). The increased weight is caused by concentric left ventricular hypertrophy that leaves almost no cavitary lumen. The myocardial cut surfaces are red-tan with no infarctions either acute or remote. The valves are thin and normally formed. The chambers have no chronic dilatation. The coronary arteries arise normally and distribute in a left dominant pattern. The left main artery is short, of wide caliber, and has 10% obstruction by soft yellow atherosclerotic plaque. The right coronary artery terminates in an acute marginal branch. It has a 70% obstructing plaque near the acute margin; the artery has compensatory dilatation leaving a 3 mm lumen. The left anterior descending artery proximally has a 50% obstruction by yellow soft atherosclerotic plaque. It has multiple soft orange plaques in the distal aspect with no more than 30% obstruction. The left circumflex artery, its obtuse marginal termination, and its atrioventricular sulcal termination have multiple 10% to 20% obstructing soft yellow atherosclerotic plaques. The endocardium is thin and has no hemorrhages.

Pulmonary: The right lung weighs 580 grams and the left lung weighs 330 grams. The pleural membranes are thin and have no lacerations. The bronchi and pulmonary arteries are patent. The cut surfaces have increased crepitance. They have moderate green tobacco staining in a centrilobular distribution, and no emphysema. The cut surfaces are tan-green-pink. They have no contusions.

Liver, Gallbladder, and Pancreas: The liver weighs 3000 grams. The capsule has a 4 mm thick fibrous rind on the right side and is thin elsewhere. The cut surfaces comprise numerous regenerative nodules of pale tan liver tissue separated by very

---

[15] This is an example of a parenthetical comment, used to insert a minor opinion in the objective part of the protocol. Segregation of the subjective and objective parts is normally accomplished by the use of separately labeled pages. The parenthetical comment is a device for prevent the opinion page from being cluttered by trivial opinions.

[16] This represents an attempt to objectify the description of the extent of the atherosclerosis so that another pathologist can gain a mental image of the extent.

fine bands of cirrhotic scar tissue.[17] The gallbladder has walls that are slightly thickened by fibrosis. The gallbladder is lined by some residual green bile and a few concretions similar to those described above. The hepatoduodenal ligament has no fibrosis. The common bile duct is not dilated. The pancreas has tan lobulated parenchyma with some postmortem lace-like saponification on its surface.

Hemic and Lymphatic: The spleen weighs 240 grams. The capsule is thin. The cut surfaces are slightly firm and are dark red. The lymph nodes are not enlarged. The vertebral marrow is dark red. The palatine tonsils are not evident. The thymus gland is partly replaced by fat.

Genitourinary: The right kidney weighs 220 grams and the left kidney weighs 250 grams. The cortical surfaces are smooth. The cut surfaces are tan and have no grit. The ureters have no dilatation. The prostate gland and seminal vesicles are unremarkable. The urinary bladder has a measured 50 milliliters of yellow urine. The testes are descended and have unremarkable stringy gray-tan parenchyma.

Endocrine: The pituitary, adrenal, and thyroid glands have no nodules, hyperplasia, or abnormal color.

Digestive: The esophagus, stomach, and duodenum have no chronic ulcers. The stomach has a measured 300 milliliters of tan partially digested food. The small and large intestines are unremarkable except for some fibrous adhesions connecting a few loops of the ileum.

Musculoskeletal: The right clavicle, the sternum, the lumbar vertebrae, and the pelvis have no recent fractures. The musculature is unremarkable except as noted.

    VIA:bh 09/08/05

MICROSCOPIC DESCRIPTION

Heart: Section of ventricular septum with chronic ischemia manifested by minimal subendocardial replacement fibrosis.

Lung: The section has bland mucous plugs in bronchi, and sheets of pigmented macrophages in alveoli. The appearances are those of tobacco abuse.[18]

Liver: Early cirrhosis; some areas have frank nodular regeneration and others merely have fibrous septa formation. The hepatocytes have macrovesicular steatosis with fatty vacuoles occupying an estimated 50% of the cross-sectional area of the liver. The cirrhotic bands are thin and have some proliferating ductules.

---

[17] Stating that the liver has cirrhosis merely gives a diagnosis; it is not adequate as a description. The simple description given here gives the informed reader some basis for making an independent opinion of cirrhosis.

[18] Because the microscopic slides are available for another pathologist to review, and because most microscopic descriptions are fundamentally opinions, the prohibition against mixing findings and opinions can be somewhat relaxed in the microscopic description, in comparison to the gross description.

Gallbladder: Chronic cholecystitis manifested by fibrosis of the wall, and lympho-plasmacytic inflammation of the submucosa. The mucosa is denuded.

[transcriptionist and date]

— End of Autopsy Report; Toxicology Report is Appended —

Appendix 3: List of Diagnoses in Case of Partially Resolved Trauma and Natural Disease

OPINION

Final Diagnosis:

Hypertensive heart disease[1]
    Left ventricular hypertrophy
    Four chamber dilatation
    Lethal ventricular arrhythmia (opinion[2])
Blunt impact to head 20 December 2004[3] (anamnestic)
    Laceration of scalp (anamnestic; healed)
    Subdural hematoma (anamnestic): nearly resolved
    Cerebral cortical contusion, resolving
Sequelae of head trauma
    Respiratory failure (anamnestic[4])
    Tracheostomy and mechanical ventriculation (anamnestic)
    Pneumonia (anamnestic): fully resolved
    Deep vein thrombosis (anamnestic)
    Swallowing disorder (anamnestic)
Aortic atherosclerosis
Cholecystolithiasis
Benign prostatic hypertrophy
Diverticulosis coli
Adrenal cortical adenoma[5]

---

[1] The diagnoses that are the causes of death are placed at the top.

[2] All diagnoses are opinions, of course. The word opinion is redundantly added here to make it clear that the diagnosis of the arrhythmia is not from any medical record.

[3] The original wounds are placed in one section, and the medical sequelae of those wounds are placed in another section. The medical sequelae are in rough chronological order.

[4] Diagnoses lifted entirely from the medical history are indicated by the word anamnestic. In this case, many of the most important diagnoses are anamnestic.

[5] Most of the morphological diagnoses in this case are of no import to the cause of death.

Cause of Death:

Hypertensive Heart Disease

Contributory Cause of Death:

Sequelae[6] of Subdural Hematoma and Brain Contusion

Manner of Death:

Accident (Pedestrian struck by light truck)

[name of pathologist], M.D.	Date Signed
Medical Examiner	

---

[6] The vital records bureau wants only the underlying condition, that is, the subdural hematoma and brain contusion. All the ensuing complications are wrapped into the word *sequelae.*

Appendix 4: Summary and Opinion Report in Case of Partially Resolved Head Trauma and Natural Cause

SUMMARY AND OPINION

Decedent: [name of decedent]   *File:* 0x-0xxxx

History and Circumstances: The decedent was an 83-year-old pedestrian struck by a light truck in a parking lot on 20 December 2004. At the hospital he was found to have a laceration of the scalp and a subdural hematoma. He developed respiratory failure for which he was treated with a tracheostomy, and deep vein thrombosis for which he was treated with a filter in the inferior vena cava. He went on to develop methicillin-resistant Staphylococcus aureus pneumonia. He improved, became afebrile, and in Jan 2005 was transferred to a long-term care hospital for ventilator management and weaning.[1]

At the second hospital he developed fecal impaction and secondary ileus. These resolved. He had a documented swallowing problem. A Doppler study showed continuing deep vein thrombosis. After being weaned from the ventilator, he was transferred to a nursing home in March 2005.

At the nursing home he received supplemental oxygen by tracheostomy. His course was unremarkable until on 19 July 2005 he was found without vital signs a few hours after being observed in his usual state of health. He did not respond to resuscitation measures and was pronounced dead.[2]

Autopsy findings: The autopsy revealed hypertensive heart disease, a healing cerebrocortical contusion, no significant residual subdural hematoma, and no residual pneumonia.[3]

---

[1] For ease of reading, the clinical summary is broken into three paragraphs; one for each treating institution.

[2] Not stated explicitly, but important to the opinion that head trauma contributed to death, is the fact that the decedent had not returned to his pre-trauma baseline at the time of his death.

[3] The recitation of autopsy findings is limited to those that are pertinent to the cause of death opinion.

Opinion: Based on the information available to me at this time, it is my opinion that [name of decedent] died as a result of a sudden ventricular arrhythmia[4] caused by hypertensive heart disease. It is my further opinion that the above-described sequelae of his head trauma contributed to the electrical instability of his heart and thereby to his death. Therefore, the manner of death is accident.

[transcriptionist name and date]

<table>
<tr><td>[name of pathologist], M.D.</td><td>Date Signed</td></tr>
<tr><td>Medical Examiner</td><td></td></tr>
</table>

---

[4] The ventricular arrhythmia is opined by the pathologist; the decedent was not attached to a cardiac monitor.

Appendix 5: Summary and Opinion Report in Case of Hemorrhagic Shock

SUMMARY AND OPINION

Decedent: [name of decedent]   *File:* 0x-0xxxx

History and Circumstances: The decedent was a 25-year-old man who on 8 October 2003 was involved in a dispute with another man over a woman. The other man stabbed the decedent and struck him in the head. At 0330 hrs paramedics found the decedent with a Glasgow coma score of 3 and a stab wound of the left upper quadrant of the abdomen. He had agonal respirations, was in sinus rhythm with a pulse rate of 68, and his blood pressure was 90/palpable. He was immobilized, intubated, medicated, and given fluid. During transport he developed bradycardia.

Emergency room physicians noted a distended abdomen and administered intravenous fluids and blood products. He was taken to the operating room for a laparotomy.

The surgeons found perforations of the left lobe of the liver, the stomach, and the infra-renal portion of the abdominal aorta. They repaired the aorta with a vein patch while continuing to administer blood products and crystalloid. The decedent developed a coagulopathy. After surgery his cardiac output decreased and his hypotension worsened despite pressors.[1] He returned to the operating room for another laparotomy. His blood pressure became negligible. He underwent a left thoracotomy and open cardiac massage. No sources of bleeding were identified, he could not be resuscitated, and he was pronounced at 0951 hrs the same day.[2]

Autopsy Findings: The autopsy confirmed the stab wound, the perforations of the liver and stomach, and the aortic repair, and revealed abrasions and contusions of the head.

---

[1] Although there is no formal opinion given as to mechanism of death, the clinical course is described well enough that the mechanism is clearly implied.

[2] The inclusion of the times of assault and death provides a temporal context for the story.

Opinion: Based on the circumstances surrounding death, review of the medical records, and the findings at autopsy, it is my opinion that [name of decedent] died from a stab wound to the abdomen with penetration of the liver and aorta. The manner of death is homicide.[3]

[transcriptionist and date]

[name of pathologist],	M.D. Date Signed
Medical Examiner	

---

[3] Stating the manner of death is optional.

Appendix 6: Scene Investigation Report in Case of Gunshot Wounds and Intoxication

REPORT OF SCENE INVESTIGATION

Decedent: [name of decedent]   *File:* 0x-0xxxx

Performed by:	[name of pathologist]	*Police Agency:*	[county] Sheriff
Location:	[street address]	*Lead Detective:*	[name of detective]
Arrival:	[date] at 0355 hours	*Informant:*	[name of detective]

Initial Background Information: The decedent was shot during a robbery attempt. Paramedics arrived, and while evaluating the decedent, turned him from a left lateral position onto his back, then back onto his left side in approximation of his original position. He was pronounced dead at the scene.

Environment: The scene is located in some parking spaces on the north side of the avenue. The area is well-lit by a street light. The ambient temperature is approximately 74 degrees and there has been no rain.[1]

Body: The body is on the pavement of the parking spaces, covered with a white sheet. The body is on its left side, and is clad in a sleeveless white T-shirt, black running pants, blue underwear, and flip-flop sandals. A moderate amount of blood is on the pavement beside the torso. A small amount of blood is on the pavement several inches to the west of the upper torso (Comment: movement of body by paramedics).

Some small ants are on the body. Rigor mortis is oncoming.[2] Livor mortis blanches with digital pressure and is consistent with position. The body is warm to the touch. Bloody liquid emanates from the mouth and nares, resulting in semi-dried blood on the face and scalp. The left pectoral region of the chest has a single-entrance gunshot wound. No soot or gunpowder is seen on the adjacent skin nor

---

[1] The environment here is a simple flat surface and merits little description.

[2] The examination concentrates on findings that will be changed by time or transportation: Signs of death and fragile evidence (flakes of gunpowder).

around the corresponding defect in the T-shirt. No wounds or foreign material are seen on the hands, other than small amounts of dirt consistent with contact with the ground.[3]

A $20 bill is found in the right front pocket of the pants. It is placed in custody of the Sheriff's crime scene technician. No other personal effects are identified.

Actions Taken: The scene is photographed. The body is turned onto a clean sheet, and the crime scene technician swabbed the hands for residue, prior to transportation.

[transcriptionist and date]

[name of pathologist], M.D.   Date Signed
Medical Examiner

---

[3] The wound is noted but not described in detail, this being left to the autopsy room examination.

Index